Helping young children with autism to learn

A practical guide for parents and staff in mainstream schools and nurseries

By **Liz Hannah**

Illustrations by **Nick Patterson**

Edition first published 2001 by The National Autistic Society

393 City Road, London EC1V 1NG

New edition first published 2014

The National Autistic Society is a charity registered in England and Wales (269425) and in Scotland (SC039427) and a company limited by guarantee registered in England (No. 1205298), registered office: 393 City Road, London EC1V 1NG.

ISBN 978 1 905722 95 2

Written by **Liz Hannah**

Original illustrations by **Steve Lockett**

New edition illustrations, based on the originals, by **Nick Patterson**

New edition designed by **Perch**

Printed in Great Britain by **Orchard Press Cheltenham Ltd**

Contents

Introduction   7

The needs of children with autism spectrum disorders   9

1. First steps – developing early communication skills   13

2. Early learning – prerequisite skills   51

3. Structured teaching   71

4. Developing literacy skills   88

5. Teaching an understanding of number   100

6. Developing social skills   107

7. Lack of imagination and flexible thought   117

8. Sensory issues   126

9: Behaviour support strategies   130

Some final thoughts   146

References   147

Further reading   149

Useful resources   150

Index   153

A note from the author

This book has been written to help parents at home and staff in mainstream schools and nurseries understand and meet the needs of children aged three to seven years who have an autism spectrum disorder. It is a practical, easy to follow guide, pulling together some tried and tested ideas to help you and the children work and play together with success.

About the author

Liz Hannah has worked for over 25 years supporting and teaching children with autism spectrum disorders in mainstream schools and nurseries. Recently, she has worked in Kenya and India training teachers and running workshops for parents to increase understanding and develop strategies that will help children on the autism spectrum.

Introduction

It has for some time now been government policy that, whenever possible, children with disabilities should have the opportunity to learn alongside their peers in local mainstream schools where they will be an integral part of their community. This is particularly effective in the early years, when children are being assessed to ascertain their needs and the amount of support and specialist teaching they may require. Over the years since inclusion began there have been a large number of specialist courses available for nursery and school staff, enabling mainstream settings to adapt to a wide range of abilities and needs.

The early years are vital for the learning of all children, but particularly for those with special educational needs. For children with autism spectrum disorders, early intervention with appropriate teaching strategies will boost the development of crucial social, communication and play skills that provide a basis for future learning. Playgroups and nurseries encourage children to learn and develop through communication, play and social interaction – all areas in which a child with an autism spectrum disorder has difficulties. However, it is important that inclusion does not try to fit square pegs into round holes, as that rarely works. Some adaptions will be necessary to ensure a child's needs can be met across all areas of development, using strategies that will reduce anxiety and make learning more meaningful to this group of children.

Many of the strategies given in this book assume that some adult help is on hand to provide extra support when needed. However, if no extra resources are available, some additional activities need only take a few minutes and can be slotted in throughout the day as opportunities arise. The important first stage is to have a good individual education plan based on an assessment of the child's abilities and to use small steps to achieve progress. Some examples of individual learning targets are included and show short-term targets that can be achieved in a few weeks. If targets are not achieved within the expected time scale, you may need to break things down into smaller steps or look at your strategies and try and come up with some different child-centred and creative ideas based on your knowledge of what the child enjoys most.

Working with children with autism spectrum disorders is often rewarding and exciting but adults can also feel challenged or confused at times. Try to find support by occasionally meeting up with others doing similar work, using the internet to find articles, advice and strategies and working closely in a team with colleagues and other professionals.

This book intends to be simple and easy to follow, and to give you varied ideas and support in day-to-day activities.

A word to parents

Although many activities in this book are school-based, much of what is suggested, particularly in the early sections, has also been written for you. Don't forget that you know your child best – the way he thinks and the things that most motivate him.

Note

Four out of five children diagnosed with autism spectrum disorders are boys. For this reason and to avoid long, convoluted sentences, this book uses 'he' when referring to a child and 'she' for a parent or teacher. However, all the information in the book applies to both sexes.

The terms 'autism spectrum disorder' (ASD), 'autism spectrum condition' (ASC) and 'autism' are used synonymously.

The needs of children with autism spectrum disorders

'Autism spectrum disorders' is a broad term that includes autism and Asperger syndrome, pervasive developmental disorder, pathological demand avoidance syndrome and semantic pragmatic disorder. It is a broad spectrum of need and includes children with varying degrees of difficulties and varying areas of ability. The number of children diagnosed with these conditions has increased rapidly in the last 25 years. The reason for this is thought to relate to more understanding of the condition and better diagnostic services.

Areas of difficulty

The difficulties children have relate to three main areas, called the 'triad of impairments':

> communication
> social interaction
> imagination and flexibility of thought.

In order to have a diagnosis, children must show difficulties in each of these areas, although autism is referred to as a spectrum because children's behaviour along each continuum is variable. Therefore, children with autism may present quite differently but still have difficulties in these main areas. In addition, many have sensory processing difficulties.

Difficulties in the area of **communication** may include:

> a lack of desire to communicate at all
> communicating needs only
> a lack of speech; disordered or delayed language
> problems with non-verbal communication relating to eye contact, gesture, expression, body language
> limited or little understanding of verbal requests and information
> good language, but with no social awareness – unable to start or keep up a conversation, only talking about own interests, failing to listen to others, assuming other people know what they are thinking and so on
> pedantic language that is very literal and shows limited understanding of idioms and jokes.

In the area of **social awareness and interaction**, children may have the following kinds of difficulty:

> having no desire to interact with others
> being interested in others only in order to have their needs met
> possibly being affectionate but on their own terms and not always at an appropriate time or place
> lacking the motivation to please others
> being friendly but with odd or inappropriate interactions
> showing little or no understanding of unspoken social rules
> having limited interaction, particularly with unfamiliar people or in unfamiliar circumstances.

Difficulties with **lack of imagination and rigidity of thought** may include the following:

> using toys as objects – for example, fiddling with the wheels on a car rather than pushing it along the ground
> being slow to develop imaginative play skills
> resisting change – for example, crying and being anxious if taken to school by a different route or becoming upset if something is arranged differently
> playing the same game over and over – sometimes based on a video or television character – and being unwilling to follow others' ideas
> learning things by rote but with no understanding of the underlying meaning
> having difficulty seeing or understanding things from other people's points of view
> following rules rigidly and not understanding exceptions
> having difficulty predicting what will happen next or recalling/reusing past experiences without visual object cues.

Other difficulties may arise from **sensory difficulties**. Many children with autism have a heightened awareness of different sounds, colours, textures and tastes that can cause them extreme discomfort. These children may be sensitive to sounds that are found daily in the classroom, like chairs scraping on the floor, and they may be troubled by sounds, colours, textures and smells that are not noticed by others. This is called hypersensitivity, and can cause a lot of distress.

Other children may seek out sounds, textures, smells and movement because they do not experience enough stimulation in those areas. This is called hyposensitivity, and a typical example is a child who wants to spin on a swing a lot, climb everywhere or jump on the furniture. These are sensory issues and need sensitive responses.

Some children with autism may also experience a range of other difficulties that are due to the way they think, learn and perceive the world. These include:

> sleeping difficulties – once they have a certain routine it is very difficult to change it
> eating difficulties – they may be sensitive to certain textures, resist trying new things and have a limited diet
> difficulties developing skills needed for independence due to problems with organisation or resistance to change
> insistence on certain rituals and routines
> fears and phobias that can include everyday things such as certain advertisements, pictures in books, specific songs or the sound of a young child crying
> weak fine motor skills or difficulty with drawing and handwriting
> poor spatial awareness due to problems with reading social cues or sensory perception difficulties
> focusing on minor details and ignoring the bigger picture – for example, looking at a spot of dirt on the floor when they are in the middle of a chasing game
> having no sense of their own or other's safety, which makes them very vulnerable
> for children with Asperger syndrome, dyspraxia or occasional clumsiness.

How difficulties affect children at school

The areas of difficulty the children experience may result in:

> a lack of understanding of what is being said
> an understanding of some words but not of the more complex meanings behind them
> difficulty listening and paying attention to the task at hand
> frequent distraction from the purpose of the activity
> a high level of anxiety when asked to attempt new tasks or meet new people
> an inability to share in a group activity due to communication or sensory difficulties or a lack of understanding of why sharing is important
> difficulty taking part in group games, with losing a game or understanding the rules of games
> a lack of awareness of others and how they may be affected by their actions – for example, snatching a toy from another child's hand
> insisting that rules are followed rigidly or that things are done in certain ways
> calling out in class or assembly
> not understanding the needs of others – for example, why it is bad to throw sand near other children
> having limited topics of conversation and talking at people rather than with them
> developing dependence on particular adults or routines

- having difficulty generalising skills they have learnt to other situations
- insisting on being at the front or back of the line or sitting in a certain place on the carpet
- showing distress if an error is made by them or someone else
- having difficulty making choices
- having difficulty talking about something that has happened in the past or putting themselves in an imaginary situation.

The key to making progress

Every child is different and has different degrees of need. The list on pages 11-12 has been written to raise awareness of the difficulties a child with autism may have that will affect the way he learns and behaves.

The key to offering good support and enabling progress where possible is to understand the individual child. No two children with autism spectrum disorders will be the same. Always be aware of the child's learning style and learning needs, and use their own interests as much as possible.

1. First steps – developing early communication skills

From a very young age, babies have been shown to imitate facial expressions and sounds made by their caregivers. For the first six months of life, parents respond to many of their baby's sounds and movements as though they have meaning: reinforcing and building up a dialogue of turn-taking and interaction using noises, movement, eye contact, facial expression and 'social timing'.
Goldbart, 1988

Children with autism spectrum disorders have difficulty in important areas of non-verbal communication. They may avoid eye contact and at times be extremely active or very self-absorbed. They rarely point to draw attention to things and share their interest with others. They may have difficulty imitating sounds, gestures or actions and attaching meaning to them, or they may imitate words and sounds heard in passing in a seemingly random way.

In the early years, communication skills overlap with social interaction skills and play. These skills build a foundation for intervention across the triad of impairments found in autism (see page 9), which include difficulties in communication, social interaction and social imagination along with inflexibility of thought. Sensory perception difficulties can also be helped using play activities though care must be taken to be considerate to each child's specific sensory needs.

The following pages include activities to develop the earliest social, communication and play skills under the following headings:

> learning to play: building a relationship with a young child
> interactive play
> strategies to encourage eye contact
> turn-taking activities to help develop early communication
> awareness of tongue and mouth
> developing an awareness of breath control
> using music to develop communication skills
> making choices
> adapting the environment to encourage communication
> developing language
> using signs and symbols.

Finding quality time together

If you are a parent of a young child, or a worker in an early years setting, you may feel there is no time to work intensively with one child. However, just ten minutes each day can be helpful. You are laying foundations for the child to begin to communicate and interact with you, a key adult. This will later extend to developing the skills for interaction with peers and other adults. Ideally, it would be easier to work in group situations, but many young children with autism in mainstream nurseries are not ready for this. They find it so much harder than their peers to cope with the noise and general demands placed on them, so a little quality quiet time can reap big rewards.

At the beginning: taking time to build a relationship

Example: Tommy is three years old and has been at nursery for a month. He has no speech and does not respond to his name at nursery, although he does look up if his mother calls him. He likes playing in sand or water but will walk away if play around the water and sand trays becomes noisy or boisterous. Sometimes he will push other children out of the way if they try to share toys he enjoys. Tommy likes to sit on the carpet on his own and listen to music, but if an adult comes to share his spot he walks away.

Target: *Tommy will sit alongside an adult and allow her to join in his play for five minutes or more.*

Young children with autism spectrum disorders may have specific interests that can be repetitive and solitary. They resist an adult or child joining in their play or only interact with an adult in their own interests, for example, loving to be chased but not chasing. Some children, especially when young, will seek out a space on their own, but others will tolerate their peers playing alongside them. In order to help and support their development in key areas, begin by developing their relationship with an adult so they allow the adult to join in and interact with them in play.

If you have a child with autism or you work with a child with autism, it is really important that you find some time each day to play together, particularly when the child is young. When the child is older it may be his peers or siblings that play this role, but adult intervention will still be needed at times.

The first step when teaching a child (let's call him Tommy) new skills is to build a relationship where he enjoys being with you and accepts that you will join in his games and activities. The time this takes will vary a lot from child to child, from no time at all to several weeks or months. If the latter is the case, it is important not to be deterred by any verbal or non-verbal 'leave me alone' message you are getting. You want Tommy to learn that you are not a threat, you are not going to rush or force him to follow your agenda. Take things slowly, developing a relationship where you are in step with him but taking his lead and interests as an entry point to develop new skills.

What you can do

Begin by sitting beside Tommy and watching him play. He may get up and walk (or run!) away every time you go to sit next to him, so it helps if you have a very motivating toy with you – for example, bubbles, a squeaking toy, spinning top, music toy.

When he accepts your presence, comment on what he is doing in a positive way. If he is playing with cars you could say 'Wow, fast car! Here it comes! Brooom!'

With a very active young child, you may want to sing happily, or quietly depending on mood, about what he is doing. For example, to the tune of *Frère Jacques* you could sing

'Tommy's jumping, Tommy's jumping,
Yes he is, yes he is,
Jumping, jumping, jumping, jumping, jumping, jumping,
Jumping Tom, jumping Tom!'

Gradually, join in with what Tommy is doing, step by step. At first, just copy what he does. It may be necessary to sit or stand alongside and give him some space. If he is jumping, start jumping alongside him but not too near, until you are sure it is going to be okay.

If he is looking at a book but does not want to share it with you, you could sit alongside with a book and say, 'I'm reading too!' Some children will allow you to share their book but you will have to look at the pages they have chosen. That is fine, because what you want to do is let Tommy become used to you sharing his space without becoming a threat.

If he is playing outside with a ball or hoop but will not let you play with it too, find a similar ball or hoop and copy what he does. If he likes to run up and down, run up and down beside him or race up and down holding hands.

When he accepts you alongside copying his actions, start to take the lead sometimes. If he always does the same thing, change it a little. Make new suggestions seem really exciting. For example, if you have been watching a music video together, start gently moving to the rhythm of the music. If you have been running up and down together, change direction and go round in circles, start blowing bubbles, or sit on the floor.

When Tommy starts to follow your lead sometimes and allows you to follow his lead sometimes, you have the start of a good relationship. Keep it up! Be enthusiastic, exciting and active. You are not only developing a relationship, you are also developing key skills, for example, joint attention, play skills, eye contact, anticipation; all essential for the development of communication and social skills.

Joint attention occurs when two or more people are paying attention to the same thing and are aware of the importance of each other in the interaction. This is a key skill, both in communication and social development and develops usually at about eight to ten months of age. This is normally the point when a baby will start initiating games with an adult, for example throwing his teddy out of his pram, then looking at the toy and then at the adult. He uses eye contact to communicate and may also laugh or make a sound. His parent picks the toy up and maybe looks at the baby and makes a comment. This is an early interactive game initiated by the baby, and it is the adult who eventually stops the game!

Lack of joint attention is one of the first signs of autism that may be present from a very young age. As a first stage towards developing joint attention, you will want your child to develop their attention skills in an interactive play activity with you.

  Target: *Tommy will show attention for at least five minutes when interacting with a familiar adult in play.*

When this has been achieved the time can be extended to ten minutes, or the target can be extended to the following.

  Target: *Tommy will show attention for five minutes or more when interacting with a familiar adult and one or two peers in play.*

Interacting together

Interactive play is any play that involves two or more participants anticipating and developing their actions in relation to each other. It is an early stage of social interaction and play skills but is also a form of communication, as each participant in the game builds on the other's actions, extending, changing and keeping the game going.

It is an important starting point to help children with autism spectrum disorder understand the importance of others and develop early social and play skills. It may feel easier to play with babies and toddlers in this way but it can also be modified to help slightly older children with autism spectrum disorders who have difficulty communicating and interacting with adults or peers.

Rough and tumble

This is the name given to games that involve vigorous activity and excitement. An adult will pick a baby up and toss him in the air. The baby will scream with excitement and lift his hands up for more. The adult does it again and the baby laughs and looks at the adult, moving his body up and down to show he wants the action repeated. 'Again?' the adult asks and the baby laughs with glee in anticipation of another exciting ride through the air.

Many types of game come into this category. You want the child to enjoy himself enough to show that he wants you to do it again. You want him to move his body, pull you, look at your

face, laugh in anticipation, make a sound or ask for more. At first you may need to prompt him. Say 'You want more?' and wait for a response. It may be a subtle flicker of the eye or a less subtle thump, but you know what it means. 'You want more!' you say and repeat the game. As the child develops his communication skills, you make it harder for him to get the desired response by moving (over some time that may be weeks or years) through some of the following stages:

> a slight movement
> a definite movement
> fleeting eye contact
> a definite look
> a sign or gesture showing what he wants
> a symbol handed to you
> a meaningful sound
> a word – 'bubbles!' or 'tickle!' for example
> a phrase – 'more tickles' – followed by a sentence – 'chase me again!'

Note that rough and tumble play is a very physical type of play. Some mainstream nurseries and schools discourage adults from touching children during play. This is an issue that should be discussed and included in special educational needs policies by nurseries and schools so that staff have clear guidelines on what is acceptable and safe.

When thinking about these issues, it can be helpful for mainstream schools to look at the guidelines followed in special school settings. It is important to remember that children who have any kind of sensory difficulty may be at a very early stage of their sensory development and need much more physical interaction with the adults around them than other children.

Rough and tumble play has to be enjoyable to the child or the purpose is lost.

Introduce different ideas gradually to see what the child really likes. Some children dislike being touched and it is important to respect this and find other ways of developing interactive play. If you are in a mainstream setting, it may be possible to use facilities like soft play equipment, PE mats and large physio balls in resource bases or special schools. Some rough and tumble play is more suited to being enjoyed at home with very small children and unless there are several adults available and a risk assessment for health and safety has been done, it is not sensible to lift and swing older children at school.

Types of rough and tumble play

Some types of play you could try are:
> giving the child a ride on your back or legs
> playing with soft play equipment – this might mean bouncing, jumping, climbing or rolling
> pushing the child gently into a ball pool or onto a soft mat
> bouncing or rolling on a big ball
> playing tickling games or blowing raspberries on ticklish places
> spinning the child round while holding their hands or waist
> playing monsters or 'I'm coming to get you!' games
> swinging or catching the child on a large piece of fabric
> playing hide and seek or peep-o under a piece of fabric or around doorways, windows and hiding spaces
> playing jump and fall-down games on thick PE mats, old sofas or any other soft surface.

Repetitive phrases, singing and rhymes are often an important part of interactive play. They help the child anticipate what is going to happen and build up the level of excitement. When swinging a young child round, you might say, 'a-one … a-two … a-threeeeee!' or, when playing chasing games, 'I'm coming to get you … here I come!' creeping up and then, when the child looks expectant, racing forward to catch them in your arms.

Two rhymes for swinging a child on a piece of fabric

You need:
> a good-sized rug, blanket or piece of strong fabric
> two or more strong adults
> a small child.

Swing to the rhythm of the rhyme and keep swinging all the way through until the last line. Say the last line slowly, building up a bit of tension, then tip the child out carefully on to a soft mat.

Bacon and eggs

One o'clock, still in bed
Two o'clock, still in bed
Three o'clock, still in bed
Four o'clock, still in bed
Five o'clock, still in bed
Six o'clock, still in bed
Seven o'clock, still in bed
Eight o'clock, bacon and eggs!

For the second rhyme, sing the words below to the tune of *The Drunken Sailor*, swinging the blanket throughout.

Hooray and up he rises!

What shall we do with Tommy?
(repeat three times)
Early in the morning?
Hooray and up he rises (repeat three times, lifting the blanket up on 'up')
Early in the morning. (swing, then say one, two, three and tip the child out, carefully, as before)

Three tickling rhymes

(Check first that the child concerned likes to be tickled.)

Bumble bee

Bumble bee, bumble bee,
buzzy, buzzy bumble bee (walk your fingers up the child's arm or body)
bumble bee, bumble bee… (pause for anticipation)
buzzy, buzzy, bumble bee! (tickle him under the chin, arm or wherever he enjoys being tickled.)

I'm coming to tickle your tummy

I'm coming to tickle your tummy
I'm coming to tickle your tummy, (with tickling fingers wriggling, gradually move closer
to the child's tummy)
I'm coming to tickle your tummy
I'm coming to tickle your tummy… (pause to create sense of anticipation)
Tickertickertickerticker (tickle tummy).

This little fish

This little fish (wriggle your forefinger)
Hid behind a rock (hide your finger)
Came creeping out… (make your wriggling finger slowly creep out)
And gave you a shock! (your finger jumps up and tickles the child)

Other ideas that will encourage early interactive play

Water play

As well as pouring water out of or into containers of different sizes and
shapes, try the following ideas. They can be used to capture a child's
interest and develop joint attention – that is, adult and child sharing
enjoyment and interest in the activity and each other. Don't always
take the lead, what you are trying to do is get a 'conversation' or
flow going between you, so that you build on each other's ideas.

Some examples of water play are:
> adding colouring to the water
> frothing up baby bubble bath with a whisk and blowing it or make shapes in it

> building a tower of blocks on a bridge across the water and anticipating the splash as they fall in
> piercing a plastic bottle in a pattern on the sides and bottom so the sand or water pours out from unexpected places – use a different bottle every day with a different pattern
> blowing bubbles with a straw in a cup containing water and a little bit of washing-up liquid or some bubble bath – this can create lovely bubbles and a lovely sound
> blowing up a balloon and floating it in the water – push it under and let it go so the air bubbles come out and try using metallic balloons for variety and durability
> filling balloons about ¼ full with water – tie them, squish and squash them
> using wind-up toys in the water, especially noisy ones such as frogs, ducks and boats
> putting cobblestones, driftwood, seaweed, shells and so on into the water and using them to create movement.

Play with puppets

The most interesting puppets are hand puppets that make a noise. If you do not have a noisy puppet, use a strong thread to sew a squeaker inside one or attach bells to the outside. Unusual puppets with bright colours, large beaks, long legs and furry textures are popular but a very simple puppet with a squeak will attract most young children.

Introduce the puppet slowly as children may be afraid of it initially. Use it to tickle, talk, dance, sing and make funny noises. Encourage the child to try it on his hand. Take turns, or use two puppets to have a conversation.

Puppets are good at the beginning and end of a play session to sing 'hello' and 'goodbye' songs. They often draw the child's attention to you and provide a good opening for other play activities. Puppets also encourage taking turns and social interaction – skills that are discussed in subsequent chapters.

Outdoor play

Push Tommy on a swing. Ask if he wants more pushes. If possible, push him from the front so that you can see the expression on his face and respond to it. To be truly interactive, you need a giant swing that has room for two, so you can play together.

Jump on a trampoline. If it is big enough, jump together; if not, stand on the side and help the child jump or jump along with him. Stop and ask the child if he wants to jump some more and wait for a response before starting again.

Play chase or hide and seek. Playing in a tunnel can be fun or hiding behind a tree or an adult's legs. This is an outdoor version of peek-a-boo and can be very exciting.

Some other ideas

Go back to 'building a relationship'. It can be hard to engage some children with autism spectrum disorders in interactive play. If you have been through the suggestions above and still have difficulty encouraging a child to play with you, try the following ideas.

Collect motivating toys and objects

These could include:
> spinning tops that play a tune
> furry animals that make a sound when squeezed
> balls that light up when bounced
> helicopters that fly up when you pull a trigger
> torches with coloured lenses
> a tape recorder with a tape of a favourite piece of music
> a Disney character (doll or puppet) from a favourite video
> a piece of fabric covered in sequins
> a helter-skelter with cars or balls
> noisy toys like drums and saucepan lids
> a piece of string, tinsel or other bright, twirling items.

Play with food

There is a good chance children will eat whatever exciting play food you give them, so if you are doing this at school, make sure the parents have signed a sheet giving permission for their child to have contact with these things. For example, you would not want a child on a strict gluten-free diet eating spaghetti or flour unless it is gluten free.

> **Cold oily spaghetti** can be great when teamed with cups, spoons and ladles and will capture the interest of most children if they can cope with the texture.

> **Raw rice and dried beans** make a lovely sound and feel good when you tip them or run your fingers through a tray-full.

> **Cloud dough** is a wonderful material made from four cups flour and ½ cup oil. Any kind of oil will do although baby oil smells the best. You can also add a few drops of lavender oil and see whether that makes the dough more attractive. This dough will squeeze together so you can make 'cakes' in moulds but it also has a wonderful texture if you just want to fluff it up or run your fingers through it. Cloud dough will keep in a sealed container until it is just too depleted or dirty to use!

> *Cornflour and water* is another magical substance that is easy to make. Tip a small box of cornflour into a tray and add water until the cornflour holds its shape when you write/draw in it. Add a little food colouring to make it more interesting if you wish. This also keeps well, it will dry out overnight and you just add water again the next time you want to use it.

> *Instant noodles, in bowls and with chopsticks*, are very popular and usually get eaten quite quickly. It is better to keep them plain and not add the flavouring unless you are sure they don't contain additives that may cause hyperactivity.

> You can make a paste with icing sugar, water and peppermint flavour. Roll into balls or roll out with a rolling pin and cut out shapes.

Talk to all the adults who know the child best. Somewhere in these conversations you will find something he enjoys that can be the beginning of a game, a relationship, and a communicative exchange. These activities will also help develop interaction with other children, providing the group is not too large.

Let the child lead

Try to have two identical toys and copy what the child does with his. If he likes playing in water, you play in water too. Do not be put off when he walks away from you – try again later. If he likes lying on his back gazing at the sky, then try it yourself! You will find some of these seemingly pointless activities enjoyable and can share that enjoyment in companionable silence.

If you reach a point where you are happy together, move things along a little. Add a variation. If you are looking at the sky, try looking at it through red glasses or a red piece of fabric. Bring some bubbles and blow them into the air. Ask another person to draw around your shapes with chalk as you lie there. Reach out and hold hands or roll across the ground.

Develop the child's interest

Some children love string and will happily sit twirling a piece for hours on end. If this is the case, collect different coloured ribbons, glittery string and pieces of rope. Tie a bell, pompom or balloon onto the end, make a snake with some cotton reels or make puppets with string for their hair. If he wants to unravel the string or chew it, you will have to judge when and how much string to allow and whether you can find a chewable substitute.

If your child loves toy cars try buying those cheap little cars that you pull back and let go. They fly across the room, providing many opportunities for anticipation, turn-taking, and games that start with ready, steady…go! Just make sure you have at least one car each.

Changing a solitary interest into two-way creative play can be difficult, but it can provide an important door into a child's world.

Making time for play

As well as grasping opportunities throughout the day to develop play and communication skills, it can be helpful to set aside a specific time each day when you take the child out of the classroom or nursery for some interactive play.

Include the play time as part of the child's daily routine, consistently signalled by a symbol, object or word. Keep some notes so that everyone knows what you have done and what responses you may be able to work on at other times. You may find it best at these times to play in an area where there are no other distractions and keep to a small number of activities.

Playmates

Although this type of interactive play initially builds on the relationship between adult and child, as soon as that relationship feels secure you should begin to include one or two other children. They can act as positive role models, showing enjoyment in interactive play activities.

Strategies to encourage eye contact

Target: *Tommy will look towards an adult to communicate his needs and interests.*

Eye contact is a natural communication skill and it can feel difficult to talk to someone if they are not looking at you. If you are teaching a child a new skill, you want to know he is paying attention to what you are saying and doing. Teaching him to look at you is an important part of gaining his attention.

Eye contact is a non-verbal skill that many children with autism spectrum disorders do not develop naturally. In fact, children with autism may feel uncomfortable looking directly at you or may not understand how hard they are supposed to look, so care should be taken to build the skill gradually and not to make it too big an issue. Accept a glance in your general direction if you feel it is an intentional look to acknowledge your presence and an attempt to communicate.

What you can do

To encourage the development of eye contact, you will need anything that might gain the child's attention and reward him for looking. You could use, for example, bubbles, balloons, puppets with bells, noisy, bright or shiny toys, cause and effect toys with switches and buttons, food or any other items the child particularly likes.

You can work on eye contact any time when there are not too many distractions, at home, at nursery or at school. Make the exercises fun by using motivating toys and rewards. Praise a good response by saying 'Good looking!' while giving the child the reward. If he steadfastly refuses to look at you, reward a near look. Many adults with autism have described how uncomfortable eye contact feels to them, so do not push it too far.

What I need

Hold an interesting toy or piece of food near your face. For instance, you may have a puppet with bells on that the child wants. Shake it near your face, saying, 'You want the puppet?' and give it to him when he looks in your direction. Blowing bubbles is another good activity as the child will be looking at your face. Hold the wand near your face and say, 'You want bubbles?' and wait for the look before blowing.

Here are some other good activities for developing eye contact.

> Play peep-o behind anything – a sheet, towel, your hands, a cupboard door or at the end of a tunnel.

> Use a big mirror to play dressing-up games, pull funny faces or put on face paint. Say 'Look at me!' and make an action or gesture when the child looks at you in the mirror – put on a big hat, make a funny noise or blow a kiss.

> Play *Row, row, row your boat*, other games or tickling games in which the child is facing you. Ask if he wants 'more' but only repeat it if he looks towards you or at you. Play chasing or spinning games but only chase or spin him when he looks at you.

> When you want to gain the child's attention – for example, if you are sitting down to do some work – say 'look at the book' and make sure you have his attention before beginning.

Activities to encourage turn-taking

Target: *Tommy will take turns with an adult in an activity he enjoys.*

Moving on to:

> Tommy will take turns with an adult and one or two peers in an activity he enjoys
> Tommy will wait his turn in a small group activity.

Turn-taking activities help build a social dialogue between a child and an adult, then between a child and his peers. It is also a vital skill in social interaction and play activities.

What you can do

To begin with, activities should be simple and very motivating for the child. It is important to remember that children with learning difficulties may take longer to respond than you expect, so give them plenty of time before prompting a response. You will be surprised how frequently a child takes his turn just as you are about to do it for him.

When playing turn-taking games it can be helpful to say, 'My turn, your turn' or 'Mummy's turn, George's turn', so the child learns to associate the words with the idea of waiting his turn. Then, when another child joins in, you can start to add to the list – for example, 'Molly's turn, George's turn, Johnny's turn' – thus building in the more complex social skill of sharing with a friend.

An object (a hat or toy) or picture/symbol can be used to show whose turn it is.

Many play activities can be shared in a turn-taking game. Here are a few ideas, starting with very simple games. Take turns:

> spinning a top or pressing a switch on a cause and effect toy (one that does something exciting when you touch it in some way, such as a music box, a toy that spins, toys that make noises when they are banged or pushed, toys that are operated with switches or pop-up toys)
> dropping balls down a tube or down a helter-skelter
> blowing bubbles, blowing a paper windmill, pouring water or sand
> rolling a car down a ramp
> laying a brick to build a tower or knocking the tower over
> playing peep-o with a scarf or piece of fabric
> dropping shapes into a posting box
> banging a drum
> bouncing a rubber ball.

More interactive turn-taking activities involve the child acknowledging your part in a game and playing with you. This can be more difficult, so it is easiest if at first you work on this in a small space with no distractions. You may need another adult to show the child what he has to do. You could try:

> pushing a car to the child and waiting for him to push it back to you
> rolling, throwing or kicking a ball and waiting for the child to return it to you – start with rolling, which is best done sitting on the floor with your legs out so there is a clear area in which to play

> bouncing or rolling a ball in a blanket or towel by holding the ends of the fabric
> hitting a balloon back and forth between you
> blow a balloon up and take turns to let it go, in the air or in water
> take turns to draw around each other's hands or feet
> have a pretend conversation on the telephone, taking turns to speak
> take turns to pour and drink a pretend cup of tea
> take turns to press a switch on a computer.

When you want another child to join in, you can try these ideas, first with an adult, then with a child or a small group of two or three:

> taking turns to turn pages and lift the flap of a book
> taking turns to go down a slide
> taking turns to squirt a balloon or target with water or paint
> playing simple games of lotto, taking turns to pick up a card
> doing a puzzle together, taking turns to place each piece
> dipping a tennis ball or marble in paint and taking turns to roll it on a piece of paper
> taking turns to hold, stroke or feed a pet
> taking turns to use an implement – for example, a rolling pin to roll dough, a biscuit cutter, an iPad or the mouse when using the computer
> taking turns in a singing game where one child sits in the middle.

Turn-taking songs

Here are three good turn-taking songs to try with a small group.

Johnny's in the garden (Chant the words with lots of expression!)

You will need:
> a fan or piece of card
> a water sprayer
> talcum powder or polystyrene chips.

'Johnny' sits in the middle while the others watch and join in the words if they can.

Johnny's in the garden *(sitting on a chair)*
Blow, wind, blow *(make some wind with the fan or card)*
Plip-plop raindrops *(spray with water)*
And down comes the snow *(lightly scatter talcum powder)*.

Don't forget to build in anticipation and drama when reciting the words!
Children really love this rhyme and can't wait to have their turn. However, some children may be distressed if their clothes get wet or dirty so do it gently at first.

Jack in the box

Sing this to the tune of *Here we go round the mulberry bush*.

You will need: a large box stable enough for a child to sit in.

Jack in the box jumps up out of bed *(child jumps up from box)*
He makes me laugh when he wobbles his head *(child wobbles his head)*
I gently push him down again *(push the child down)*
But Jack in the box jumps up instead! *(child jumps up again)*.

The hokey-cokey

One child goes in the middle of the circle while the others stand in a circle around him.
The child in the middle could wear a special hat or scarf.

Put Joseph in, put Joseph out *(lead the child in and out of the circle)*
In, out, in, out
And tickle him all about *(tickle or shake him)*
You do the hokey-cokey and turn around *(wriggle hips and turn around)*
That's what it's all about.

Other children then take their turn at being in the middle.

Awareness of tongue and mouth

Some non-verbal children may not be aware of their tongue and lips and what they can do, although they are very important for forming sounds. Exercises that help to encourage oral awareness and movement of the tongue include the following:

> sticking your tongue out and asking the child to copy you – when he can stick his tongue out in imitation, develop this by asking him to imitate you in moving your tongue up and down and from side to side around your mouth
> putting honey or jam on the child's lips and round his mouth so that he will lick it off with his tongue
> blowing out your cheeks and seeing if the child can copy you
> blowing raspberries with your lips and asking the child to try and copy you
> doing a 'native American battle cry' in which you make a high 'whoop' and move your hand on and off your mouth at speed
> blowing kisses
> putting lipstick on and making kisses on a mirror
> licking a lollipop or pretending to lick an ice cream.

Developing breath control

Breath control is also important for developing and controlling sounds. Exercises you can use to develop breath control include:

> blowing bubbles with a bubble wand or through a straw
> blowing or sucking through a straw
> blowing a whistle or kazoo
> blowing dandelion clocks
> blowing boats on the water
> blowing frothed up bubble bath off their hands or yours
> blowing feathers
> blowing on a mirror or window and making a pattern
> blowing candles
> blowing paper windmills to make them spin.

Using music to develop communication skills

Most young children love music and sometimes their language first begins to emerge as the words of a song. Singing can make unpleasant tasks more enjoyable, help develop play, soothe and give pleasure.

If you do not know many simple children's songs, it is possible to buy or borrow suitable CDs and DVDs from the library, often with a book which provides the words and actions to accompany the songs. Also, a lot of children's songs and actions can be found online on YouTube and on children's channels. It is possible to buy an excellent set of books online that include songs using 'Makaton' signing, which is a simplified version of British Sign Language. Short, repetitive songs are best, so the child learns phrases, learns to anticipate a word or action and wants to fill in the gaps at the appropriate places. Whether you choose to teach Makaton signs or stick to actions or a combination of both is up to you and the communication policy at your school.

What you can do

Target: *Tommy will anticipate an action in a familiar song.*

Moving on to:

> Tommy will imitate an action/sign in a familiar song
> Tommy will join in the actions/signs in a familiar song
> Tommy will fill in a missing word in a familiar song
> Tommy will sing a familiar song and do the actions/signs.

Try making up songs to describe your actions or those of the child. A 'singing commentary' about a child's play can be a good way to join in, comment and develop a turn-taking dialogue. Copy the child's actions sometimes, then change the sound a little bit and see if he will copy you.

Sing a song with actions – for example, one in which the child gets tickled. When the song is familiar, leave a gap before the action to see if the child will ask for the tickle or make a movement to show anticipation. Make sure the gap is long enough to give the child plenty of time to respond, but not so long that he loses interest in the tickle.

Sit facing the child or have the child facing you on your lap. Sing simple nursery songs and, when they are familiar, leave out key words or phrases to encourage the child to fill in the spaces. Make a big thing of this, leave a gap, look expectantly at the child, give him enough time to respond but not so long that you lose the rhythm of the song completely.

Do not give up if the child does not respond – keep up the expectation that he will fill in the gap with a sound or gesture. It often happens when you are not expecting it.

A good song for copying a sound, action or word is *Row, row, row your boat*.

Row, row, row your boat

Row, row, row your boat, gently down the stream *(have the child facing you, hold hands and row back and forth)*
If you see a crocodile, don't forget to scream AHHHHH! *(scream!)*

Row, row, row your boat, gently down the river,
If you see a polar bear, don't forget to shiver. BRRRRR! *(hold your arms across your body and give a good shiver)*

Row, row, row your boat, gently round the lake
If you hear a hissing noise it's probably a snake (SSSSSSS!) *(make a loud hissing sound)*

Sometimes children will only sing on their own, stopping when you join in. Do not worry about this. Try to join in gradually, singing along to the last line or very quietly.

You could also try recording or filming the child while he is singing and playing it back to him. This helps him develop an awareness of his voice and what it can do. Children usually enjoy hearing themselves in a recording or seeing themselves on screen, although they may be confused at first.

Songs can be a good way to teach imitation skills. Say you have a sound or an action and want the child to copy. First, show him what to do and prompt him if necessary. Then, gradually withdraw the prompt and see if he will copy the action by himself.

You can also use simple actions, such as clapping, banging drums or shaking shakers and get the child to copy your action. This then becomes a good turn-taking activity.

Here are two good songs for developing imitation and turn-taking skills.

Johnny can you do this?

Johnny can you do this, do this, do this *(use the child's name in place of 'Johnny')*
Johnny can you do this
Just like me.

Johnny can you clap your hands, clap your hands, clap your hands, *(your turn)*
Johnny can you clap your hands,
Just like me.
Clapping, clapping, clapping, clapping, clapping, *(child's turn to join in)*
Clapping, clapping, clapping,
Just like me.

Johnny can you bang the drum, bang the drum, bang the drum,
Johnny can you bang the drum
Just like me.
Banging, banging, banging, banging, banging,
banging, banging, banging
Just like me.

Put your hand on your head

(Sing this to the tune of If you're happy and you know it.)
Put your hand on your head, on your head,
Put your hand on your head, on your head,
Put your hand on your head, put your hand on your head,
Put your hand on your head, on your head.

Put your hand on your nose, on your nose … *(and so on)*

Put your hand on your tummy, on your tummy *... (and so on)*

These and similar songs can also be used to help teach body parts and body awareness.

There are a few more strategies that are also very worthwhile. Relaxation tapes, for example, are useful to help you relax with a child and spend some gentle time together. Start with a short time and always use the same music, so the child knows it is time to relax. Lie in a comfortable place – preferably a darkened room or quiet area – and let the music wash over you. A specific cushion or blanket can be used to show the child it is time for relaxation.

Some children love certain songs from favourite DVDs or songs they have heard on the television. These are very useful to have on tape or CD as a reward or for times when you want the child to be calm – for example, in the car.

Making choices

Offering choices to children is a good way to help them learn how useful communication skills can be. It also helps give them a sense of purpose, of having some control over their environment.

> **Target:** *Tommy will take a preferred item when offered a choice of two items.*
> *For example, food, drink, toys, books, clothes, pencils or DVDs.*

Moving on over an extended period of time to:

> Tommy will take a preferred item when offered a choice of three or four items
> Tommy will match a photo, picture or symbol to a familiar item
> Tommy will choose a preferred item when offered two photos, pictures or symbols of those items
> Tommy will choose a preferred item or activity from a choice board.

At the beginning you may need to start by offering a favourite item and something you know the child does not like. However, as soon as he has grasped the idea of choosing, you can offer two favourite items to choose from. If you are asking the child to make a choice between snacks, for example, hold them up and say clearly, 'You want a <u>biscuit</u> or <u>crisps</u>?' emphasising the words as you do so. If he always chooses biscuits to have for his snack, but you know he likes apples and bananas, try taking the biscuits away altogether and offering a choice between the two types of fruit. This may cause difficulties at first if the child is used to having biscuits, but, after a few days, he may be able to cope well with choosing alternatives and accepting them happily.

There are many opportunities throughout the day to offer choices. At first, do not offer more than two choices at once, as this could be confusing, but make the choices meaningful. If a child at home independently takes the DVD he wants to watch, make this a better communicative opportunity by putting them away out of sight and just offering a choice of his two favourites. He may grab both, (or he may have a tantrum!), but you can prompt him to point to or take one. If he still grabs at both DVDs simultaneously, keep them at different distances apart and give the first one he touches. He may be upset at first but will soon learn that he has to choose the one he prefers.

When a child can match pictures to objects, and understands that pictures can be used to represent real objects, you can also use pictorial choice boards. For example, make up cards with copies of pictures from the covers of the DVDs and teach him to choose by pointing to the appropriate card or by taking the card and handing it to you (see the section on the Picture Exchange Communication System and using symbols, page 48). Symbols, drawings, photographs and copies of packaging can all be used to make choice boards but do not clutter them with too many choices at first. If your child always makes the same choice, leave that picture card out sometimes or put a cross over it to show that it is not available.

Bubbles

Balloon

Good times to offer choices

Start by holding up two cards, then increase the number of choices. These could be:

> choosing between toys, DVDs, books or CDs, for example asking 'You want the animal book or the monster book?' and when the child reaches for a book, saying, 'You want the monster book. Okay, we'll have the monster book', then putting the other book away
> choosing between snacks and drinks or choosing a filling for a sandwich, colouring for icing on a cake, which cutter to use for playdough or cookie dough
> choosing between songs and games – you can have a picture for each song and put them on a board so the child can choose the one he wants
> choosing items of clothing – for example, plain socks or patterned socks
> choosing an outing – feeding the ducks or going on the swings
> choosing colours for colouring, beads for threading or wooden building blocks – for example, asking 'You want the red pen or the blue pen?' or 'You want the round bead or the square bead?' or 'You want a big block or a little block?'

Adapting the environment to encourage communication

In most homes and nurseries, children's toys and activities are not placed on high shelves or in locked cupboards. They are readily accessible so that children can learn by exploring. However, for young children with severe communication difficulties, providing easy access to everything they need removes important opportunities to teach them to communicate with others and show how rewarding such communication can be.

Adapting the environment to provide more opportunities for communication needs to be planned carefully. You do not want to make things more difficult by putting favourite toys in tantalising view but on a high shelf, resulting in the child making a dangerous climb to reach it. Similarly, in a nursery, there may be little you can do to change the general environment. However, even given these kinds of constraints, there are many little things you can do throughout the day to help develop communication skills.

Children with autism spectrum disorders may ask for what they want by looking at something, pointing, dragging you towards the object, standing under or beside the cupboard or shelf where things are kept, crying, speaking aloud (but not always asking somebody) or having a tantrum. Consider how the child communicates his needs and try to move him on to the next stage by teaching pointing and the use of eye contact or by using symbols, pictures, sounds or spoken words.

What you can do

When you first try the ideas that follow, the child may be perplexed and become frustrated very quickly. However, if you model the correct response before he becomes upset, he will soon begin to understand what is expected and some of the things you try will become little jokes between you.

> Keep favourite toys and food in a locked cupboard. Stick symbols, photographs or pictures on the cupboard using Velcro and teach the child to bring you the picture of the thing he wants. This can work well for DVDs, snacks and favourite toys. If you do not want a child to have a particular toy or snack, you can remove the card or place a red cross over it.

> If a child is able to ask for what he wants but seldom does so, symbols and picture cards will help him understand that he has to go to an adult and ask for them. You can then encourage him to use a word, phrase or sentence to do this, depending on his language ability. You should always emphasise what the child has said – for example, if he says 'book', you reply, 'You want the book. Let's get the book.'

> You can set up situations where you 'forget' to give the child something important, like giving a cup for a drink but not putting any drink in it or not giving a spoon at dinner-time when you know he has his favourite dessert and will need a spoon to eat it. Sometimes you may have to prompt a request if the child cries or sits silently but give plenty of time for him to ask for himself. A communication book or board that contains pictures, symbols or written words (if the child can read) can be a very useful prompt for a reluctant speaker.

> You can also try giving the child something that is wrong – a pencil with a broken point or a plastic biscuit instead of a real one, for example – or do something wrong – such as trying to put a sock on a hand instead of a foot. Whatever you do, make sure that you give enough time for the child to respond, and try to choose things that are motivating for him.

> When you are playing a game or doing a favourite puzzle, keep a piece in your hand and see if the child responds by asking for it.

> When you give a child something he wants, do not do so all at once. If you have crisps, keep the packet and hand them over one at a time as he requests them. Similarly, if you have balls for a helter-skelter, dolls in a doll's house or pieces for a posting box, keep them and wait until he asks for the next one. The request may be in the form of a look, gesture, symbol, word or sentence – whatever level of communication you are working towards. You may also need to teach 'no' so the child is able to tell you he does not want any of the choices available. A symbol with a red cross, a sign or the word 'no' can be taught to the individual child, as appropriate.

See also the section about the Picture Exchange Communication System on page 48.

Developing language

Some health authorities provide excellent speech and language therapy support. These professionals will assess each child's needs and provide suitable activities and strategies to help language development. In general, language strategies are aimed at developing functional language, which means that children are helped to develop language skills in the classroom or at home while doing activities that are part of their daily routine. This includes play, daily routines such as mealtimes, story time, bath time and varied activities like trips out, cooking, singing or artwork. In fact, most things that children do throughout their day can become opportunities to develop their language with a little adult support.

The ideas given overleaf can help children to develop language while doing other activities.

What you can do

Working with children with minimal vocabulary

The following are some ideas for how to work with young children who are vocalising but have minimal vocabulary.

> Use language clearly in a happy voice. People speak to babies in a sing-song voice and this is helpful to all children who are developing language. It helps make your message clear if your voice is expressive and you sound interesting.

> You should always stress the main words.

> Sing familiar songs and rhymes and leave a sudden gap before the last word or phrase to see if the child will anticipate by making a sound or saying the word. For example, you could sing 'The wheels on the bus go round and round, round and round, round and round, the wheels on the bus go round and round, all day long.' With this song, you can leave out the last word of a line or the last phrase, 'all day long', which remains the same throughout all the verses in the song. Make the end exciting, by looking in expectation, maybe with a gesture or mime for the child to respond.

> When looking at books with a child who is still at an early stage of language development, choose picture books. You can point to the pictures and use words as labels.

> There are some wonderful storybooks for young children that have repetitive phrases on each page. When your child knows the story, leave out the last word or phrase and see if he will say it. Do not forget to show anticipation in your voice and wait for several seconds so that he has time to respond.

> Play games in which you are using the same word or phrase. Leave the last word out and see if the child will fill it in – for example, 'Ready, steady, go!' 'One, two, three!' Always say the last word with great enthusiasm, clearly making it important.

> You can make car and animal or other relevant noises when playing or reading books. You can say 'Wheeee!' when the child goes down the slide,

'Brooom brooom!' when he pushes a car, 'Mooo!' when he plays with a cow puppet. *Old Macdonald had a farm* is an excellent song to encourage a child to make sounds.

> When doing an activity such as posting shapes, you could say 'gone!' as each shape drops through the hole. When the child is used to this routine, leave a gap to see if he will fill in the word. Or take turns and see if he will say 'gone!' on his turn.

> When playing on the slide or climbing frame, use words to describe what the child is doing but stress one word – for example, '<u>Up</u> the ladder!', '<u>Down</u> the slide!' Alternatively, you could simply say 'up' and 'down', repeating the words with an up and down expression and gesture. You also have opportunities to practise these words when playing with cars, play people or a doll's house. Work on particular key words and make sure that all adults interacting with that child know which words to emphasise.

> Use opportunities to label things the child is using and stress the important words. Make sounds interesting – for example, 'Yoghurt! Yum, yum!'

> If a child is using a number of single words, try to extend them into familiar phrases by using adjectives – 'big bird', 'yellow pencil', 'dirty hands'. Introduce the words as often as possible in everyday contexts. Verbs can also be added to nouns to make longer phrases – 'drink milk', 'eat the biscuit', 'Jack's dancing!' for example.

> Encourage the child to use short phrases by using words such as 'more', as in 'more drink', or 'gone', as in 'drink gone'. Repeat the word or phrase whenever suitable opportunities arise. Use gestures to support what you say.

> Many children with autism spectrum disorders are echolalic, which means they repeat whatever is said to them. They often do this when they are not sure what is meant, but it is a good start because you know they can say the words and you can use the fact that they will copy you to encourage and extend their vocabulary. Use a lot of repetition, with the same phrases being built into daily routines until the child begins to understand what he is repeating and give it meaning.

Ideas for children who are using sentences

Some children may be able to speak quite well but are not able to have a conversation or give information that is not related to their own interests and needs. They do not have the idea of language as social interaction and cannot understand that you may be interested in something they did if they themselves are no longer interested in it.

They may also have difficulty recalling information and need a visual or verbal reminder of an event that has happened in the past (which may be five minutes ago) in order to talk about it.

The ideas given below can help develop the skills of these children.

> Try sending the child on a small errand with another child or adult and then ask him to tell you about it. At first you may have to prompt all the answers or use visual prompts, but, after some practice, he will be able to tell you what he did in two or three sentences.

> For example, you ask the child to go to the office with the classroom assistant to take the register. On his return, you pretend to have forgotten what you asked him to do and say, 'Where have you been?' The answer may need to be prompted – 'To the office'. 'Why did you go to the office?' to which he replies 'I took the register'. 'Who was in the office?' you say and 'Mrs Jones' is the reply.

> After a time, you should be able to withdraw the prompts and the child may begin to volunteer more information spontaneously. Returning with a visual cue or object (a written message, a book) may prompt the conversation.

> Give a child a toy or object and ask him to tell you three things about it. He may tell you 'It's a cow' and you will have to prompt the rest by asking what colour it is and how many legs it has, or what sound it makes. However, in time, you will be able to gradually withdraw the prompts.

> It is useful to have visual prompts to help a child tell you about something he has done. You could ask his parents to send in some reminders of what he did at the weekend. For example, if he went shopping and then went to get a burger, he could bring in a shopping bag and a burger wrapper.

On school trips and special school activities, it is particularly important to have a photographic record and examples of what the child has done so he can tell others about it. A visual reminder of a trip to the seaside could include shells, a train ticket and some sunscreen. Include anything that will trigger memory and help the child talk about his experience.

For a more verbal child, you could practise having conversations that you start, rather like a turn-taking game. You could have a microphone that goes back and forth to encourage the conversation and emphasise whose turn it is. You say the opening line, the child then makes a comment and you go back and forth until you run out of things to say. Better still, play it as a game with one or two other children, where they have to have a conversation and you give them the first line. You may need to prompt the answers at first:

'I like playing football.'
'I like playing on my computer.'
'I played football at the weekend with my dad. He said I was good at kicking.'
'I played Star Wars on my computer with my brother and I won.' (and so on)

Using stories to develop language and communication skills

There are several ways in which you can use stories to develop these skills. For example:
> using picture cards and storybooks to encourage language development
> retelling stories with different characters or a different ending chosen by the children
> when reading a story, asking a question about what might happen next
> using language to describe the characters, for example, good, bad, naughty, happy, sad, messy, lost, found, scary or friendly
> looking at pictures in magazines and books and talking about what you see – use 'Why?', 'Where?' and 'Who?' questions, for example, 'Why is the car dirty?' 'Why is the girl wearing a helmet?' What has happened to the dog?' 'Who has eaten all the porridge?' 'Where is the goat?'

Some children find these questions very hard to answer and may need prompting. They will find 'Why?' questions particularly hard as they have to use inference, which is difficult if you can't imagine things from someone else's point of view. If children have difficulty answering questions about pictures, try using photographs taken in the playground and on outings or ask questions about real situations. For example, try writing with a broken pencil and say, 'Why won't my pencil write?'

If you have access to a camera, this is a very good way to present a visual reminder of an event that has just happened and has many benefits for language and learning. For example, a simple science experiment could be photographed and the pictures used to encourage written and spoken language, sequencing and to reinforce what has happened in the lesson. Pictures can be uploaded onto the computer, and words or symbols added, or they can be made into books and wall displays.

Using signs and symbols

Target: *Tommy will follow simple instructions given with symbol support, eg 'sit down', 'be quiet', 'cut', 'draw', 'get your coat' or 'listen to the teacher'.*

Why use signs and symbols?

Signs and symbols support spoken language and help develop communication, language and literacy skills. When you speak to a child with communication difficulties, whether or not he understands will depend on the context in which the statement was made, the tone of voice in which it was said and non-verbal communication cues, such as body language and gestures. If a teacher says 'Line up', and all the children stand up and go to line up, the child will follow, as this is a routine that is repeated several times a day. If a mother goes to her child, points to his feet and says 'Get your shoes', he will run and get his shoes because she has pointed to his feet. He knows he has to put his shoes on before they go out and he is very motivated to do what her gesture indicates because he always enjoys going out.

Children with autism spectrum disorders may pick up on contextual cues because they are tuned in to routines and know what happens within them. However, that does not mean they have understood the verbal instruction or even that they understand the reason for doing what they are asked. A child will line up with the others in his class, but his idea of where he is going might be based on previous knowledge of familiar routines. He may think it is dinnertime and then be very distressed when he finds himself in assembly. Some other communication system is essential to help this child understand what is going to happen and to support the spoken word.

Even children who have good vocabulary may have difficulty understanding exactly what they have been told or asked because they are unfamiliar with the context or because background noise affects their ability to process what has been said. Therefore, especially with young children it is always helpful to use symbols to support key instructions or information. If a child can read, written information is also a good support to spoken language. Teachers must be aware of the gap there may be between expressive and receptive language, ie between speaking and understanding.

Signs or symbols?

Children with autism spectrum disorders have difficulty reading body language and facial expressions and often have poor eye contact, so looking at a person when they are speaking can be difficult for them. For this reason, it is usually easier to use symbols rather than signs to support language and teach communication skills. However, signs can be used to support routines – for example, to show a child he is going to be taken to the toilet or is being asked to sit down or come to the teacher. Similarly, gestures can be used. Indeed, exaggerated gestures can be very helpful, even when the child is not looking, as he may see them in his peripheral vision and respond accordingly.

Children often learn one sign and use that for everything. Signs taught at snack time may include 'biscuit' and 'please' or 'thank you', which are easy signs to prompt and do. It is important to note that it is not a good idea to teach children to sign or to say 'please' and 'thank you' when they have a very small vocabulary as they will use it to ask for everything they want and will then have difficulty learning names, signs or symbols to communicate their needs. Use opportunities to develop and extend communication skills, not to make it too easy.

Using symbols

Symbols are line drawings with written words at the bottom. You can use your own drawings, pieces of packaging or pictures cut out of books and magazines. However, once you have the computer software (and most schools do now), it is easy to make symbols of any size and to use them at home and school. They do not require specialist knowledge and, as they have the word written under the picture, they can be used to support literacy skills as well as language skills.

Children with autism spectrum disorders often have good visual awareness. Temple Grandin, a woman with autism, has written about how she sees things in pictures. She describes how she sees concepts by picturing an example of that concept (a hot fire). To read more about this, see Temple Grandin's book *Thinking in pictures* (see page 147). This, and other examples from writers with autism, support the view that symbols are a good choice if you are looking for a communication system for a child with autism.

Symbols can also be used to give meaning to written information for children with poor literacy skills. For children who can quickly decode writing and read well but not with meaning, symbols clarify what they are reading and make it easier to understand. Many children who become fluent at reading with symbols can cope very well if the symbols are changed, particularly if it is something concrete like 'car' rather than something abstract like 'as' or 'the'.

Children who have fairly good language skills but delayed literacy skills find symbols can give them confidence in reading so that they begin to have greater success in reading words. Texts can then be written with a combination of words with or without symbols. Symbols make abstract texts more accessible to children with literacy and comprehension difficulties and they can also type or dictate their own work using a symbols programme and read it back to their teacher, parents or peers.

Picture Exchange Communication System (PECS)

This is a system of teaching communication skills to children who have autism spectrum disorders. It was developed in the US by psychologist Andrew Bondy and speech and language therapist Lori Frost and is now used by schools and by speech and language therapists throughout the UK. The system is very intensive to begin with, as two adults are needed, and it is taught at home, school and used everywhere the child goes.

Frost and Bondy found that using PECS had the unexpected outcome of helping children to speak, as well as giving them a communication system that is easy to use. This means children feel less frustrated and more in control of their environment, giving the additional benefit of making them calmer and happier.

Film/DVD

Drink

Apple

Bubbles

Want

Biscuit

PECS can be used with any child who is not using language to communicate. This includes children who have some words but do not use them consistently or in a communicative manner. Thus you can use it with a child who will, for example, feel thirsty and say 'drink' while standing alone in the playground looking at his feet.

PECS teaches children to be active partners in a communicative exchange. They are taught to take a symbol to an adult to ask for something they want. When they are proficient at doing this, they are taught to use concepts ('I want the big biscuit'), adjectives ('I want the clean car'), numbers ('I see three fire engines') and to comment on things they hear ('I hear a telephone'), see ('I see a yellow duck') and feel ('I feel thirsty'). PECS can also be used to encourage communication between peers and support the development of turn-taking and play skills.

PECS should be taught by adults who have been trained to use it correctly. If it is not, children can become dependent on physical and verbal prompts that will prevent them developing spontaneous communication skills.

It is now possible to buy software for tablets that will speak when a button is pressed. Each page might look like a page in a PECS book but it is easier to use as it is quicker to set up, requires little strength or co-ordination, symbols don't get lost and a tablet is much more compact than a whole book of symbols. Most software can be programmed with a familiar voice, or the child's own voice. For details of where to find symbols and software, look in the Useful resources section at the back of this book (page 150).

2. Early learning – prerequisite skills

It is important when a child with an autism spectrum disorder starts nursery or school to assess their strengths and needs in order to draw up a short individual education plan as soon as possible. You may have a speech and language therapist, specialist teacher or educational psychologist to help you. If you have to wait for these services, and you have a child with complex needs, it can be daunting knowing where to start.

Where you start will depend on the child's age, ability and the setting you are in, but the first section in Chapter 1, 'Finding quality time together' and 'At the beginning: taking time to build a relationship' (page 14), is a good beginning for a young child. It is important not to wait too long for the child to 'settle' before setting short-term targets because during the settling period children may develop expectations and patterns of coping behaviour that will be difficult to change. If you find the child develops skills faster than you expected, it doesn't matter – it only takes a short time to set new targets. Remember, small steps are best, then important skills are not overlooked.

This section suggests the following strategies to develop early skills that are important for learning:

> using rewards and praise
> teaching a child to sit down
> teaching a child to wait
> motivating a child
> developing attention and concentration
> developing imitation skills
> modelling and prompting
> forward and backward chaining
> generalising skills and knowledge.

Using rewards and praise

Children with autism may not have an in-built desire to please others. They often do not understand why they should do something they do not want to do. They may feel anxious when asked to do something unfamiliar and prefer to do activities they know and enjoy, that feel safe and help them feel secure.

To encourage children to complete tasks you want them to do – particularly if the task is unfamiliar or difficult for them – it is often necessary to give a reward. At first the reward must be something that is very motivating, so, for young children it may involve giving them a favourite toy or food item. Initially it should be something that can be given frequently and taken away (or eaten) in a very short time. If food is the only reward that seems to work, it can be broken into very small pieces so that children are not being filled up with junk food between meals. Some children have particular interests that can be used as a reward for doing what you want. For example, if Ben completes his writing satisfactorily he can look at the big book of flags until playtime. This can be shown visually using symbols placed along a Velcro strip.

Rewards should always be given together with praise. When you praise a child, you must look and sound happy so the child understands your meaning even when they do not understand the words you have said. Praise should be clear and precise – for example, 'Good looking!', 'Good sitting!', 'Very good try!', 'Great drawing!'

Rewards and praise should be given immediately after the child gives the correct response or completes the activity satisfactorily. A child can be rewarded for working by being told they can 'go and play' or go to the computer or to some other favourite activity. He should know that when he has completed the task he will get the reward and this may be put on his timetable at school or on a visual chart at home.

As children grow older, more sophisticated systems of rewards can be put in place as they learn to wait for their reward. They could have tick charts or sticker books where they have to fill a certain number of boxes and are then given a special reward. The chart or book should say clearly what the reward (token, tick, sticker) is for and this should be explained verbally or visually. The child must be able to see how many tokens he needs in order to earn his reward. At first it may be two or three during a single lesson, but an older child may be able to wait until the end of the day or week. This system works best when parents are also involved and encourage their child with interest and praise. It is important that reward charts and sticker books are designed to allow bad days to happen without upsetting the child's motivation and making them feel the reward will never come. Do not take stickers away for bad behaviour but be positive in your expectation that, although today was terrible, tomorrow will be better.

Sometimes, if a child is really struggling, you can have a two-layer system of rewards, so there is an ultimate reward and a slightly less exciting reward, which should also be shown visually on a chart. This strategy is more successful with children who can understand clearly the reasons why the best reward has not been reached that session (or that day).

See also Chapter 9: behaviour support strategies (page 130).

Teaching a child to sit down in a quiet area of the classroom

When a child with an autism spectrum disorder comes into nursery or school, one of the first things he will need to be taught is to sit down when asked. The school environment will be particularly stimulating for him, as he may have heightened sensory awareness and find the sounds, smells and colours in the room quite overwhelming. He may not understand why he should sit down when the other children do or feel that it is important to please the teacher and do as she asks. However, sitting down is a very important skill to learn and a prerequisite to many early learning activities at school and at home.

Target: *When working in a quiet area with an adult, Tommy will sit on a chair for one minute when requested to do so.*

Moving on to:

> when working in a quiet area with an adult, Tommy will sit and attend to an activity for five minutes
> when working in a quiet area with an adult, Tommy will sit for 15 minutes and complete one or more work tasks with adult support
> when working in a quiet, familiar area Tommy will sit and complete a familiar task independently, with minimal adult support
> Tommy will sit in a small group and complete a familiar task independently.

When a child is sitting, he is more able to focus on what is in front of him and is less likely to become distracted by other things happening around him. He also knows that when he sits, he is expected to do something: listen to a story, draw a picture, do a puzzle or cut some paper, for example. A table and chair create a boundary around him that is important for a young child in helping him to pay attention to the task at hand.

What you can do

Begin by having a suitably sized table and chair in a quiet area of the room. Have some very motivating toys on the table and see if the child will sit by himself to explore the toys. If not, try a little prompt – pat the chair and say 'Sit down.' Praise the child if he sits by saying 'Good sitting!' and immediately show him what wonderful things you have.

Some children will run up to the table, take the most exciting thing and run away to play with it. You will then have to take the toy, say 'My turn.' in a firm voice and try to tempt the child back to the table to play with the toy. Sometimes you may have to show him what is expected by sitting him on the chair and immediately rewarding him with the toy and the phrase 'Good sitting!'

Gradually build up the time you expect Tommy to sit, from a few seconds to eat a snack or flick a switch, up to 20 minutes or more to complete a number of activities you want to work on with him. For a school-age child, you will eventually want him to sit for the same time as his peers, although he will often need some work adapted to meet his learning needs.

Sitting in groups

Target: *Tommy will sit on a chair or the carpet for five minutes with an adult lightly supporting him.*

Moving on to:

> Tommy will sit on the carpet for ten minutes with an adult nearby giving minimal support
> Tommy will sit in a small group for five minutes and join in an activity with adult support
> Tommy will complete a familiar activity independently in the classroom alongside his peers.

Learning new skills in a group situation can be difficult for young children with autism spectrum disorders. They may be sensitive to the closeness of others around them and feel uncomfortable. In assembly, large echoing spaces can make them feel panicky. They may not understand what is being said by the teacher, that the teacher is talking to them or that they are expected to listen quietly and pay attention. They may feel they have to sit there forever, which will make them feel anxious.

Chapter 2: Early learning – prerequisite skills

Here are some ideas to help a child learn to sit in a group.

> Sit the child on the edge or at the front of the group near the teacher.

> A very young child may need to sit on a chair against an adult's legs at first. When he is used to the routine of sitting on the carpet, he can gradually be moved onto the floor or a chair.

> If a child is restless sitting on the carpet, sit him on a chair with an adult sitting in a small chair behind him, lightly holding him.

> Some children find sitting in a large group is easier if they know where to sit. If it is practical, have a mat or cushion marking where they should sit on the carpet.

> Remind the child verbally and visually (using a symbol or gesture) to sit quietly and listen.

> If the teacher is reading a story, try to give the child a copy of the book or a toy that symbolises the story, such as a teddy bear or doll to represent Goldilocks.

> Use gestures and physical and verbal prompts to help him join in with songs.

> When asking questions, remember that a child with an autism spectrum disorder may not realise he is expected to answer unless he is spoken to by name. Therefore, use his name to get his attention before asking the question. Remember, too, to get his attention before making a request. If you say his name at the end of the sentence it may be too late and the question will be lost.

> If you have a child who disturbs others in the group during carpet time, (and if you have enough help), consider taking him out with one or two other children and covering the same topic with more direct teaching and sensory input. For example, make a story more real by illustrating it with things to hold, smell and feel, or slow down the pace of a maths lesson by using real examples.

> In assembly, sit a child who may become distressed or distracted on the end of a row so he can leave easily if he is having difficulty sitting still. A small chair or cushion may be necessary to show the child he should remain in one place.

> Have clear targets for the child and gradually build up the time he is expected to sit in a group. If he has poor language and listening skills and does not understand what is happening in assembly, what are you hoping to achieve by having him sit there? Is he ready to learn to sit quietly and listen in a large group? Is it helping develop his social interaction skills? If not, and there is somebody available to work with him in the classroom, it may be a good time to do some individual work in language or other basic learning skills instead.

See also Chapter 3: structured teaching (page 71), and Chapter 9: behaviour support strategies (page 130).

Teaching a child to wait

Children with autism spectrum disorders sometimes have difficulty understanding that something is going to happen in the near future. They think that if it is not happening now, then it is not going to happen at all. This can make them feel anxious and, in some children, the anxiety and frustration can result in a tantrum or aggressive behaviour.

For example, Tommy understands that it is nearly lunchtime as he can read the cues around him. However, he wants to start his lunch before he has sat down and will have a tantrum if he is prevented from doing this. He is hungry, anxious that he won't get his lunch and then inconsolable.

> **Short-term target:** *Tommy will wait until he is sitting down before he opens his lunchbox.*

> **Long-term target:** *Tommy will wait calmly for an hour or more for an event or activity to happen, eg going to the shop or going swimming.*

What you can do

The best way to deal with this is to teach Tommy to wait. You will need a 'wait' symbol, which should be large and brightly coloured with the word 'wait' written on it. Cut out several that are identical and laminate them, as they will be needed in any situation where Tommy has to wait. Have at least two at school and several at home – perhaps one in each room of the house (especially the kitchen) and one in the car. Put some time aside every day to teach the concept of waiting.

To begin with, it is best to use a very motivating reward, such as bubbles, a spinning top or other sensory toy that makes sounds or has flashing lights. Show Tommy what you have and ask if he wants it. For example, say 'Blow bubbles?' and blow lots of bubbles. When he shows he wants more bubbles say 'Wait' firmly and, at the same time, put the wait card in front of the child or give it to him to hold. Start by counting to five then say, 'Good waiting!' and blow some more bubbles.

Check your child has understood the instructions. Some children with autism spectrum disorders have good vocabulary but still have difficulty following complex instructions or instructions that are given to a group.

With a young child, remember to make rewards immediate. Gradually increase the time he has to wait for the reward or the number of ticks he has to collect in order to get it, so that as he gets older he can wait for the reward to come at the end of the day or week.

Work closely with parents. They will tell you if something has upset the child before coming in to school or if he slept badly. You can then subtly make fewer demands or build in more relaxation time to allow for this.

Developing attention and concentration

There are many reasons why children with autism might have difficulty paying attention in the classroom. They may have heightened sensory awareness so that certain everyday sounds, colours, smells and textures will fascinate, distract or disturb them. People with autism spectrum disorders who have written about their experiences often talk about their sensory difficulties and how uncomfortable and overwhelming they can be.

What you can do

Here are some things you could try to help increase a child's concentration span.

> Sit the child in the least distracting area of the room, away from the door and the computer (see Chapter 3: structured teaching, page 71).

> Try not to shout! It can be very distressing for a child with an autism spectrum disorder and it can confuse him. If your voice rises at the end of a sentence, that may be what he responds to even if the beginning of the sentence was 'I told you not to … '.

> Be sensitive to the child's needs when introducing new experiences. He may need a gradual introduction to paint or dough, music or PE. Do not give up, but take it step by step, offering plenty of encouragement.

> Try to organise a regular place for him to go if things in the classroom get too difficult for him. A session in a corner of the classroom, listening to a tape through headphones, can be enough to block out difficult noises and calm the child down.

Another important reason for a child exhibiting poor attention and concentration could be a lack of interest in what he is doing. Although some children with autism spectrum disorders want to emulate their peers and follow school rules rigidly, others may not want to do anything that does not fit within their range of interests.

You can try making these small practical changes:

> make rewards very motivating and do not make the child wait too long for a reward
> ensure the child knows how much work he has to do and what is going to happen when he has finished
> if possible, adapt the work to include the child's interests – for example, if he loves trains and is learning to use a number line, make the number line into a train with carriages or even a railway line
> take things step-by-step and build the work up at a pace that suits the child.

Attention and classroom skills

Some children with autism may not realise what is expected of them in the classroom. They will not know, unless it is made very clear to them, that they should listen to the teacher. They might think the teacher is talking to the other children, not to them. They might not realise when they should start work and how much work they should do. It is also important to realise that they might not have understood the verbal instructions given by the teacher or that they perhaps have difficulty remembering a sequence of instructions.

If this happens, try the following techniques.

> Using the child's name and pausing before giving the instruction is the best way to make sure he hears what you say. For children with good language skills, you may be tempted to use longer or more complex sentences, but only do so if it is necessary.

> When the teacher is talking, you could give the child a visual reminder to listen to what is being said. This can either be a symbol (a drawing), a sign (hand cupped around your ear) or a written reminder.

> Use concrete examples where possible, particularly with young children.

> Keep verbal instructions brief, stressing the main words. If a child can only follow one verbal instruction at a time, it is important to give the instructions one at a time.

> Make sure the child can see what he has to do and check that he has understood. If he can read, it is better to write the instructions down in a list. He can then cross off each step as it is completed.

> Use a lot of praise, especially with younger children. Use phrases like 'Good sitting!', 'Good looking!', 'Good writing!', 'Good work!' and so on.

If a child will not settle

We all have a bad day sometimes. If a child with autism is having a bad day and is very inattentive, it may be better to give him a break than to make the situation worse by waiting until he has disrupted other children and created an incident in the classroom. If he is in reception, could he do something relaxing in the nursery for a while? If he has adult support in class, could he go for a walk, on an errand or to the library? Maybe he could take his work and finish it in a quiet, empty room. Whatever you choose to do, do it calmly before there is a crisis.

It is important not to take the child away from his work and give him something that is normally given as a reward. Try to find other distractions, if that is what is needed. The reward must be earned, although it is perfectly fine to give it for effort rather than success. We all know that sometimes a small task can require huge effort if we are having a really bad day.

See also Chapter 3: structured teaching (page 71), and Social Stories™, page 114.

Developing imitation skills

Children learn some new skills by copying others. This is difficult for many children with autism spectrum disorders. They may learn to copy things that fascinate them, like favourite scenes in Disney videos, or things that are odd and have caught their attention, like the way their baby sister eats her porridge, but they have difficulty copying important things like language, play and social interaction skills. You may stand in front of a child waving and saying, 'Wave bye bye!', but the chances are he will look puzzled and fail to respond or make an attempt that is not quite right.

The most important thing is your awareness. If you remember that you have a child who has difficulty copying you, then you will not depend on it when teaching a new skill. Some children with autism spectrum disorders will copy their peers rigidly as they like things to be fixed and orderly. However, they will often copy without understanding so they still need extra help to make their actions meaningful.

What you can do

With young children, play games in which you copy their sounds and actions and see if they respond. The child may be taken aback and look as though he has just noticed your presence. When you are sure you have his attention, copy him and change it a little to see if the child will copy you. (See Chapter 1, 'At the beginning: taking time to build a relationship', page 14).

Try making exaggerated sounds or doing things that are funny, such as pulling faces in the mirror, pretending to be a ghost or blowing raspberries. Have two similar hats that are noticeable because they are very big, very bright or very furry, for example. Put your hat on and look in the mirror. Then give the mirror to the child and see if he will copy you with the other hat.

In a more formal learning situation when you want a child to copy, always use short phrases and clear language. 'Do this' is a useful phrase in this context, followed by a clear example of what you want the child to do. The child learns that 'Do this' means 'Copy what I am doing.' You may say 'Clap!' or 'Wave!', demonstrating the action or including it in a game or song. You may need to use a physical prompt to teach the child what to do and gradually withdraw the prompt.

Chapter 2: Early learning – prerequisite skills

It is important to remember that teaching a child to copy is not the same as teaching the meaning of what he is copying. When children learn by imitation, it is the social context in which they learn it that teaches them a great deal more than the physical skill alone. They will be learning how others respond, what they expect and what meaning it has. If you say, 'Do this,' and wave, and the child copies you, he will still have to learn the social context of waving. This includes, for example, that it is a way of saying goodbye: you look at the other person when you do it and the other person usually says 'Goodbye' and waves back.

Even with a verbal child, it is better to keep complex language to a minimum as the child will find it easier if you give an example of what he is supposed to do, rather than a lengthy verbal explanation. If you are teaching him to sort fruit into apples, pears and oranges, you can demonstrate what to do by simply using the words, 'apple', 'pear' and 'orange' and show where the fruit has to go. You may extend this by saying 'apple with apple', 'pear with pear', but do not be tempted to give a longer explanation. For example, this instruction given at normal speed, without a visual example, could overwhelm a child who is already struggling to cope with too much sensory input: 'Now... you have to put all the apples together in the red dish and all the pears go together in the green dish and the oranges have to go here in the orange dish. Do you think you could do that for me?'

Children who have difficulty drawing are often able to do so if you draw the picture bit by bit and they copy it step by step. First of all they would need to copy straight lines and circles. Then start a person with the head, body, arms and legs. Finally, when they can copy a stick figure independently, they can learn to copy the eyes, nose, mouth, ears and hair, step by step. For many children, this practice develops over months or years into wonderful creative drawing of their own. It can be helpful if you each have an identical piece of paper, but if you are using an easel or computer, you can divide the paper in half with a thick line and do your drawing on your half so they can see clearly that there are two sides – one for you and one for them.

This strategy can also be useful when teaching construction or matching skills. Here, you sit facing the child and give a step-by-step example. Then, the child sits and copies each step until he has learned what to do independently. There is no creativity in teaching skills this way, but you can work up to that by turning your copying activity into a turn-taking game, in which you each place a piece on the item you are building and see how it turns out.

Repetition is important, especially with a young child. You may think that he is never going to drink that pretend cup of tea or wave goodbye or draw a picture. One day, though, it will happen – often when you are not watching.

Prompting and modelling

Prompting, modelling, and shaping are techniques that can be used to teach skills in a structured, step-by-step process. They are particularly important for children with autism spectrum disorders because they are clear and have success built in. For example, if you want to teach a young child to pedal a trike, you may find it more difficult than you expect and give up quite quickly. You think the child is physically capable of pedalling but he makes no progress. This might be because he does not understand what is expected, why he needs to do it, or he may have difficulty co-ordinating his body or understanding the process (pushing on the pedal will make the trike move). He sits on the trike and plays with the bell or rocks back and forth on it a few times and then gets off. You know that, if he could learn, he would have such fun, independently pedalling around the playground or park.

Prompting

In order to teach a child how to pedal a trike, you will need to use a physical prompt. In other words, you put his feet on the pedals, put your hands over them and push them around. Do this slowly, as much as the child will tolerate each day, until he gains confidence. As you push his foot down on the pedal, also use a verbal prompt – 'Push! Push!' Then, gradually withdraw the physical prompt by making it lighter, so the child has to use more effort to pedal, but not so light that he gives up. It should then be possible to withdraw the physical prompt and just use the verbal prompt until the child can pedal with no help at all.

However, if he clearly isn't ready for this and gets distressed, leave it for another time. Never use physical prompts when a child is afraid, instead think of other new skills that may be more acceptable, like jumping on a trampoline, climbing steps, or using various classroom tools and toys with switches and parts to manipulate. The technique can be used for teaching many physical skills. The hardest but most important thing to do is to withdraw the physical prompt as soon as possible – otherwise the child can become dependent on it. A verbal prompt is a good initial back-up, but it can also gradually be withdrawn or replaced by a sign or gesture.

Modelling and shaping

This technique is used for children who are able to copy what you do. You show the child what to do, then ask them to copy you. If they are unable to copy you or make an error, you may want to show the skill again or use a physical or verbal prompt to help them complete the activity successfully.

It is always helpful when teaching a complex skill, like making a rocket out of junk, to have a completed model handy as an example. Children will then feel a lot more confident to have a go themselves. You can model each step for them and support them as they copy you at each point. You can take photos and make a book that can be used as a reminder and a topic for discussion, as well as a record of the child's work.

Shaping occurs when you change a child's skills or behaviour in small steps to reach a desired target. For example, if he always makes circular marks on paper, you can show him how to draw a circle, then a face, then other circular drawings like an apple, a cat or a snowman. If he likes making the sound 'mamama', you could start by copying the sound and change it to 'mum' then to 'mummy', or if he waves his hands to music you might show him how to clap. Shaping is a natural response when teaching young children and should be used consistently with plenty of praise at each new step.

Hand over hand

If you are working with a child who does not mind being touched, some skills can be taught by putting your hands over the child's hands and doing it with him. This can be helpful when teaching skills that require manipulation and fine motor skills, such as taking lids off pots, using switches, using a knife and fork or using a pencil or paintbrush.

Again, it is important to gradually withdraw the prompt, so the child can do the last step unaided, then the last two steps and so on.

Forward and backward chaining

Forward and backward chaining is a technique for teaching new skills, particularly to children who have difficulty with organisation skills, attention or language. The aim is to break the task you are teaching down into smaller components, making sure the child achieves success before becoming frustrated.

Forward chaining

This technique is used when you break things down into small steps and teach the child the first step in the chain. When he has mastered the first step, you teach the next step and so on. For example, if you want to teach a child to tie his shoelaces, you will teach the first step of crossing over the laces and then finish tying them yourself. When the child had mastered crossing the laces, you teach him to make the first loop, then the second and so on. At each stage, praise his progress and he will feel he has achieved something positive.

Backward chaining

This is used when you teach the last step in a chain first, so the child has the pleasure of successfully completing a task. When teaching a new puzzle, say, you put all the pieces together except the last one, which the child successfully puts in place. You then do all but the last two pieces, which the child does, then the last three and so on until he is able to complete the puzzle by himself.

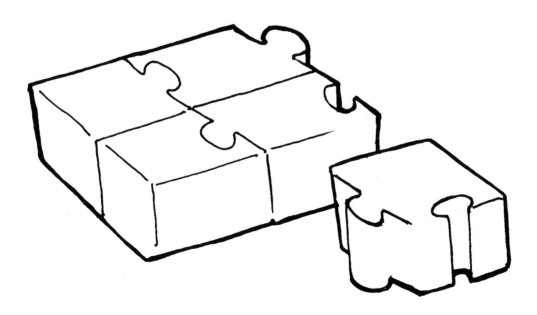

Backward chaining builds confidence and is rewarding for the child. It is possible to teach many skills this way. For example, threading beads is a complex skill that requires both hands to work together. It is easier to teach the child to pull the lace through a bead before teaching him how to thread the lace into the bead. You can divide the task into steps:

> you hold the bead and push the lace in, the child pulls it through
> you hold the bead, the child pushes the lace in and pulls it out the other end
> the child holds the bead, pushes the lace in and pulls the lace out.

Each stage might take some time for the child to learn. Do not keep going over the same thing week after week if he is not progressing at all and you feel you are not moving on. Look for other activities that are easier and may be a 'stepping stone'. In the example given of threading beads, try lacing toys, cotton reels, threading on to a dowel, threading pasta and different sizes and shapes of beads.

Sometimes it is easier to teach a skill in a different order to the one that follows naturally. If it is easier to do it this way and it will still give the child a sense of accomplishment, then go ahead and do it. The important things to remember are:

> break the task into small steps
> teach the child one step at a time
> use visuals (photos or simple line drawings) if possible and appropriate
> be consistent – do not have a different adult teaching the child to use a knife and fork in a different way every day
> make sure success and rewards are built in to the process
> use a lot of praise.

Generalising skills and knowledge

Children with autism spectrum disorders are very rigid in their thinking. This means they have enormous difficulty transferring what they have learnt in one situation to other similar situations. Parents will say, 'She always eats with a knife and fork at home' and this will be news to the teacher, who will reply, 'That is strange – she doesn't seem to know what to do with a fork here. We have difficulty stopping her eating everything with her fingers.' Equally, further discussion may reveal several skills the child has learnt at school – undressing and dressing for swimming, for example – that the parents did not know their child could manage independently. This lack of ability to generalise one skill or piece of knowledge to other situations can be a serious difficulty when the teacher is not aware of it.

What you can do

What you do depends to some extent on the level of the child's understanding but, essentially, it is important to always generalise what you are teaching across a wide number of relevant situations and examples.

For instance, you may be teaching language skills. You have a lovely picture of a house and teach the child 'This is a house.' You have to make sure that the child knows what real houses look like and that they come in all shapes and sizes. Picture books often show country cottages with sloping roofs, a smoking chimney and flowering climbers growing up the wall. However, many children live in terraced houses or blocks of flats that do not look at all like this.

Teaching in mainstream schools depends a great deal on the premise that children will quickly generalise what they have learnt across a wide number and variety of different situations. Make sure the child with an autism spectrum disorder has opportunities to learn the same thing in different situations, beginning with a range of practical and relevant examples. If you have a child who can only subtract using small wooden blocks, he will need to practise that same skill using practical examples in different settings before moving on to learning more complex ideas.

Make sure that there is good communication between teachers, carers and parents so that children can practise new skills at home, at nursery or at school. A notebook that goes back and forth from home to school can be very helpful in keeping everyone up to date.

3. Structured teaching

The idea of structured teaching is one aspect of the approach set out in Treatment and Education of Autistic and related Communication-handicapped Children (TEACCH) which is based in North Carolina, USA. It is used in many forms in specialist schools and units for children with autism spectrum disorders throughout the UK, adapted by teachers, parents or carers to suit the requirements of the child and the situation in which it is used.

The most important aspect of structured teaching is that the child can see exactly what the task is and what will happen when it is finished. He has a schedule showing the order of activities and tasks are presented visually so that he is clear on what has to be done. For a very able child, this may mean that he has a written list of instructions detailing the task or activity. For a young child doing a sorting task, it may mean that there are several objects to sort and a visual prompt such as coloured bowls or bowls of different sizes to show how they should be sorted. Tasks and activities are based on the child's skills and needs and taught in a step-by-step way so that important prerequisite skills are not missed out.

Using structured teaching reduces anxiety and improves attention and motivation. It also discourages a high level of dependence on an adult. Organising work visually so that a child with autism can see what he has to do and so he is not distracted by unimportant details is always important and should be kept in mind whenever work is presented.

Structured teaching is particularly useful when you:

> have a distractible, inattentive or unhappy child
> want to teach a child to complete a task or series of tasks independently
> want to teach a new skill and the child is having difficulty understanding what he has to do.

Structured teaching is useful at home too – particularly for teaching independent dressing and washing skills. In nursery, it helps calm an excitable child and provides a focus to learn new skills and work on specific developmental targets. As the child gets older, it helps develop independent working skills so he knows what is expected and does not constantly need an adult by his side.

The next few pages about structured teaching contain information under these headings:

> developing and using timetables and schedules
> how structured teaching is organised
> meeting the needs of a child with autism spectrum disorder in nursery or playgroup.

Developing and using timetables and schedules

Many children with autism spectrum disorders need to know what is happening now and what is going to happen next. They find change difficult to deal with and can be distressed by unexpected events and cancellations. They often have difficulty organising themselves and can feel extremely anxious when faced with the unknown.

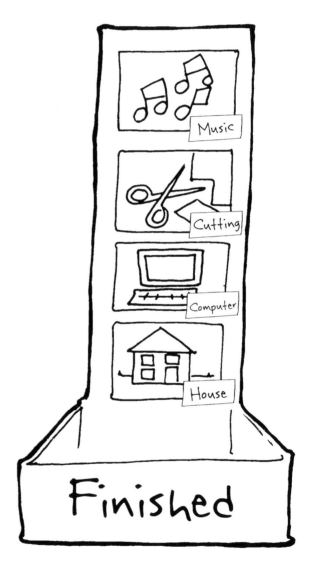

Timetables and schedules are therefore useful at home and at school. A child at school who is familiar with the routine of the day will feel more relaxed when he can see it laid out in pictures or words in front of him. A child at home will have a structure to his day and will not feel he is 'freewheeling' through time in a haphazard manner.

Timetables and schedules can use photographs, symbols, drawings or words depending on what is easiest for each child to understand. The most important aim is to have something clear and unambiguous that does not give too much information at once. The timetable or schedule can be written in list form on a sheet of paper or lined up on a strip of card. A schedule can be used to break down the school day or a single activity into manageable steps. It can be used at home to show the routine of the day, help organise and structure busy times or teach particular skills.

Making a timetable for a child in a nursery

Velcro is a wonderful invention that comes in very handy when you want to make a timetable for a young child. Make sure you laminate the symbols, photos and drawings you want to use so that they are tough and can be used time and time again.

For a young child starting nursery, a timetable using clear symbols or line drawings is best. The first thing to do is teach the child what the symbols mean. This can take several weeks, so start with a very simple timetable and use it consistently every day.

The different areas the symbols relate to should also be labelled with larger versions of the same symbols. So, the outside play symbol can be placed on the outside door, the milk and story symbol in an uncluttered space near the carpet, the home symbol near the exit and so on.

Have the pictures for the main activities of the day lined up from top to bottom or from left to right on a piece of card. The top five centimetres (two inches) of the card should be a different colour to the rest and it is helpful if you can make a small box or pocket at the bottom to keep the finished cards together. If not, a posting box or plastic wallet next to the timetable will do just as well.

You may have the symbols shown in the picture running from top to bottom on the timetable.

For terms such as 'inside play' and 'outside play', use a drawing of a favourite toy or activity used at these times.

At the beginning of the session, show the child his timetable, which should be somewhere accessible on the wall and away from visual distractions. At first, just talk about the top symbol. When the child understands the timetable, you can then point to each symbol and explain what it is.

Jo's timetable

Inside play

Work

Outside play

Milk and a story

Home

For children who enjoy looking at photographs, you may want to have a photo of the child doing each activity instead of (or as well as) the symbols. However, make sure the photographs are clear and unambiguous, as a child may just look at one thing in the picture (for example, bubbles) that is not available every day.

Take the first activity symbol to the activity area and match it with the big symbol there. When the activity is finished, you go back to the timetable with the child and, saying 'Play finished', place that symbol in the box or pocket at the bottom or the plastic envelope fixed to the wall beside it. You then pick up the next symbol and show it to the child, saying 'work' and take it to match with the symbol in his structured work area.

If two activities run into each other and occur in the same place, such as milk and story, it is okay to put them on the same symbol or just to use one symbol that applies to both activities – maybe a circle of chairs.

If an activity is changed (outside play is not possible because it is raining very hard, for example) make sure that the symbol is changed on the timetable as soon as possible. Also, put a large red cross over the large outside play symbol that is on the door to the outside play area to show the child that there is no outside play today. This does not always calm the child, particularly a young child, and so other strategies may have to be organised in advance.

A cancelled swimming session can be particularly distressing and you may need to think in advance how to prepare the child for this and what activity can be used to replace it. Social Stories™ (see page 114) can be helpful in preparing the child for understanding what will happen if swimming is cancelled.

Note that, as a child learns what each symbol means, there is no need to match it to the various areas. Just have a different colour of card at the top of the timetable and place the symbol there.

Many children with autism spectrum disorders who are in mainstream primary schools seem to manage very well without a timetable. They follow what the other children are doing and do not want to do anything that will make them feel different. However, if there is a change to their usual day or if they have a supply teacher, they may feel very anxious and find it difficult to concentrate. They may become difficult and disrupt the class. Teachers can avoid this by having a clearly-written class timetable on the board twice a day at registration. If there is a last-minute change, it is then very easy to alter it and the child then knows what is going to happen. This may also help other children in the class.

At home, schedules can be an enormous help for encouraging a child with an autism spectrum disorder to organise himself. For example, they can help a child to get dressed and be ready for school in the morning or with the bedtime routine in the evening. In the same way, many children like to read television programme guides even though they know very well when their favourite programmes will be on. Having the guide gives them extra reassurance that nothing has changed.

This technique can be used to help with other weekly activities and outings, such as shopping, youth club, drama class and so on. It can be reassuring for the child to have a weekly schedule of these posted up somewhere. Use words, drawings or photographs – whatever is easiest for the child to follow – and be sure to keep it up to date. Think how you would feel if you lost your diary or forgot to put in important changes to plans.

You can use schedules and lists to teach independence skills. For example, below is a list of instructions for a boy who can read well but gets very muddled when he has to use the toilet. He pulls off far too much paper and leaves it lying around the toilet. He gets in a mess and forgets to flush the toilet or wash his hands. Try writing a list like this and you realise just how complicated some things we do every day really are!

After doing a poo:

> stand up
> pull the toilet paper down to the red line
> tear the paper off at the green line
> bend over and wipe your bottom
> put the paper in the toilet
> take more paper down to the red line
> pull the paper off at the green line
> wipe your bottom again.

Lists and schedules giving instructions should be tried out several times with an adult to make sure the child knows what to do and check that the instructions are clear and unambiguous. It is surprising how difficult it can be to give clear, step-by-step instructions to a child who is unlikely to fill in any obvious omissions.

Other visual aids can also be used. In this case, the toilet roll holder is marked with a green line on the serrated edge. A red line is marked about 46 cm (18 in) down. The child is taught how to pull the paper to the red line and tear it at the green line, wipe his bottom and follow the instructions, which are stuck on the wall at eye level. Instructions like these can help other children too.

How structured teaching is organised

Example 1

You have four-year-old Jackson in your nursery who flits around the room touching some things but rarely attempting anything new.

He likes to do puzzles and is so fascinated by numbers and letters he will spend a large part of his time gazing at posters of the alphabet and number displays.

You do have a special needs room, but he spends all his time in there looking at the number line on the wall. You want to move him on, but how can you do it?

What you can do

Make up a timetable with pictures, photographs or symbols showing the main events of the day. Include a 'work' symbol or photo.

Find a work area inside the classroom that has few distractions. Use screens, the back of shelving units and the wall to make the area as bare as possible. When Jackson is used to sitting there, he can begin to personalise it with his work.

> You will need two trays or boxes (in different colours) and five plastic wallets. Put two small pieces of Velcro on each plastic wallet and put a strip of Velcro on a piece of strong card.

> Have two sets of numbers, '1' to '5', laminated, with Velcro on the back. In addition, have a symbol or picture of something that Jackson really enjoys – in this case, an alphabet book.

> Stick one set of numbers in a line on the strong card and one number on each of the plastic wallets. Put the reward symbol after the '5'.

> Put one activity in each plastic wallet. Put exactly what Jackson will need in order to do that activity and no more. For example, if you only want him to have a choice of three coloured pens, just put three in. If you want him to thread five cotton reels, just put five in.

> Nothing should be confusing or ambiguous. Children with autism spectrum disorders find it hard to know what is important and what is not. They can feel overwhelmed by a large number of colours, sizes and shapes and will not know where to start.

> Put all the plastic wallets, in order, in one box or tray. This is the 'work' box. Green is a good colour for this box.

> Put an activity Jackson is able to do at the beginning. This helps him to settle down and achieve success early on.

> Set up the work area with the work box on the left and the 'finished' box on the right. The strip of strong card with the numbers '1' to '5' on it should be in the middle where Jackson can reach it. The numbers can go from left to right or from top to bottom. Some children will not be able to match numbers so they should have five coloured simple shapes to match instead.

> Take Jackson to his timetable and show him the 'work' symbol before taking him to sit at his table. If possible, you should sit opposite him so he can see your face and follow your example. If that is not possible, sit beside him. Show him how to take the first card from the strip, match it to the first wallet in the work box and do the activity. When it is completed, prompt him to put it in the finished box. He then takes the second card and so on until he has completed all the activities.

> At first, you will have to show Jackson what to do by modelling and prompting. Keep your language clear and brief, using a lot of praise and stressing the main words – 'Match the card', 'Open the bag', 'Good writing', 'Finished'.

When you first introduce structured teaching, you may have to reward Jackson after every completed task. The reward should be something that does not take long and will not be distracting. Coloured spinning tops that light up are good or some bubbles. The big reward comes at the end, when all the tasks have been completed.

With a young child, it is most useful to use this structured time to teach new skills. When he has learnt a new skill, encourage him to practise it in the nursery alongside other children or in a small group. Generalise the skill using different materials or introduce it into a different context. For example, if he has learned to thread beads in the structured work sessions, teach him to thread cotton reels, pasta, plastic shapes and so on alongside his peers to make necklaces, belts, wiggly worms, Christmas decorations and so on.

Some children learn new skills very quickly using this method of teaching. If so, keep changing the activities in the structured sessions while ensuring they are being practised in the classroom. Even a short structured session of 20 to 30 minutes every day can be enough to calm a child, teach new skills and improve attention and concentration throughout the day.

Example 2
Joe is in Year Two and has adult support throughout the day. He has autism and dyspraxia and is dependent on his support worker. Although his language and social skills are developing well, he is not able to read or write without the help of symbols.

Joe's memory is poor, he is dreamy and easily distracted by others. He likes to spin things and manages to find all kinds of things to spin when he should be working. When Joe's support worker is away, he is left on his own to daydream and spin or is taken to the nursery to 'help', although this usually means he chooses an activity he enjoys and plays repetitively by himself.

What you can do

It is important that Joe learns to work independently. Every day, he should do some independent structured work that will help him practise skills he needs but does not find too difficult.

> Give Joe a work area in a quiet corner of the classroom. Have his work prepared for him so that he knows what to do and use symbols to support brief written instructions. Make sure he has what he needs near at hand or give him a pictorial list of what he has to collect.

> Gradually build up the time that Joe spends doing independent work. Start with ten minutes, then, as he achieves this, add five more minutes and so on until you have reached a time that seems reasonable for him.

> Give him enough work to fill the allotted time. Use a number strip as described above or use maths, writing, reading and other symbols. Put each workbook or activity in a plastic wallet in a work box and have a finished box too, as described above.

> Joe needs a very motivating reward. A good reward could be an extra special spinning toy that he is allowed to spin for ten minutes when he has completed all his work. He could also have a reward book from which he chooses his reward.

> It might be helpful to organise his work time so he gets some extra minutes of reward time if he finishes his work quickly and less reward time if he is very slow. He has the ability to understand this.

> Joe should also be encouraged to work with a group using peer support. He is able to read using symbols and can complete worksheets that require cutting, sticking, colouring, matching and joining pictures and dots. He can fill in the initial letter of words. As he becomes more used to working independently in his own work space, he will be able to transfer these skills to a group situation.

Example 3

Lily is seven years old and has autism. She attends her local primary school and is able to read simple texts.

She likes to do what the other children are doing, has good imitation skills and is not distracted by noise or activity. With some help from the teacher and her peers, she is able to cope independently in the class for a large part of the day.

At home, however, she is not so independent. She has two younger siblings, aged five and three, and there is always a rush in the morning because Lily will not wash or dress herself for school so her mother has to do it for her. Physically, there is no reason for Lily not to be dressing herself as she manages to change for swimming without help and at school she will change for PE. There is plenty of time to dress herself in the morning, as she wakes early and goes downstairs to turn on the television. This has been encouraged by the rest of the family so that they can have a little longer to sleep.

What you can do

Lily's parents will have to get up at the same time as Lily to teach her to follow a routine. However, when she has learned what to do, she will be able to manage independently.

> Lily should have a timetable showing the order of things she needs to do in the morning. This can be made using pictures and words or just words.

> The activities (shown here with a symbol and the word) are stuck with Velcro to a strip of card and she takes each one off and posts it in a finished box when she has done it.

> Lily is given two baskets in her bedroom. One is labelled 'pyjamas' and one is labelled 'clothes'.

> In the evening, Lily's clothes are placed in the basket in the order she needs to put them on. Using backward chaining (see Chapter 2, page 67), she is taught that, in the morning, she is to take off her pyjamas, put them in the pyjamas basket and put her clothes on from the other basket. She still needs help with her shoes and socks so these are done later.

> In the bottom of the clothes basket is a big television picture. Lily learns that when she has reached this she is allowed to watch television.

> If Lily is watching television in her pyjamas when her parents get up, it is turned off and she is taken to her timetable, shown what she has to do and told to do it. If she makes a fuss, it is ignored. She is always praised when she gets herself dressed.

Lily morning schedule

Toilet — Pyjamas off

Clothes on — TV

Breakfast — Wash

Brush teeth — Brush hair

Socks and shoes on — Coat on

Book bag — School

> When it is time to have a wash, Lily has two more baskets in the bathroom. One is labelled 'wash' and one 'finished'. In the wash basket is a flannel, hand towel, toothbrush, toothpaste and, at the bottom, a picture of a hairbrush. Using backward chaining, Lily is taught to wash herself in the morning with minimal help. When she has washed, her mother gives her some hand cream as a reward as Lily loves to rub it on her hands.

Wash   Brush teeth   Clothes on   Socks and shoes on

At weekends and holidays, Lily has the same routine (dress first, then watch television), as she is not yet able to distinguish exceptions to the rule. However, once she has become comfortable with her dressing routine, she can be given a visual timetable each day, showing which days she has to get dressed before she watches television and the days when she can get dressed after breakfast. This will help her understand that days are different and not to become too insistent on having the same routine each day.

Lily enjoys going to school so that is a reward in itself. At weekends and holidays, she has a reward book that she can choose a reward from when she has completed all the tasks on her schedule.

What these examples show

These three examples show some of the ways in which structured teaching can be used to help teach children with autism spectrum disorder. It can help teachers and parents manage difficult behaviour in the classroom and at home because the children are calmer, they know what is expected and what is going to happen next. Although the technique depends on a motivating rewards system, as the child becomes older and more confident, it is possible to introduce ticks or stickers, which they have to 'save up' for a reward.

Structured teaching can be adapted to most situations. Teachers in mainstream schools sometimes worry that it isolates the child from his peers. However, everything has to be a balance between meeting the child's complex needs and helping him learn alongside others. A child who constantly depends on adult help in order to feel secure or is unable to settle in a noisy classroom and focus on learning new skills needs structured teaching, but it should not take up the whole day.

Meeting the needs of a child with autism in nursery or playgroup

Example 4

A three-and-a-half-year-old boy with autism has started at the nursery where you work as a teacher. You have wide experience of working with children with special educational needs but have never worked with a child with autism before.

You have been with the nursery nurse to meet the child, Yusef, at home. He has severe social and communication difficulties with no language and will make his needs known by pulling an adult towards what he wants or bringing a cup for a drink. He manipulates toys but does not play in a meaningful way, although he enjoys pushing switches repeatedly on musical cause and effect toys.

Yusef will do a familiar 12-piece inset puzzle unaided, although he cannot sit still for more than two or three minutes and will constantly leave an activity or meal to run up and down the room several times. His favourite activities at home are watching the music channel on television and running about at the park.

His parents say that although his gross motor skills are good, he tends to push other children out of the way if they are climbing the slide when he is or if they are in his path when he is running about. He does not realise the implications of hurting another child and will ignore the commotion he causes and carry on with what he is doing.

Yusef will be at nursery for two and a half hours each day. He will have 30 minutes of daily support from a learning support assistant who has no training in autism, although she has worked with a child with a loss of hearing. His parents have requested a statutory assessment of his special educational needs but they have not heard whether or not it has been agreed. He is on a waiting list for speech and language therapy. How can you help him?

What you can do

If possible, organise some training for staff in the nursery in autism spectrum disorders. Find out if your local authority has a specialist teacher for children with autism spectrum disorders, a specialist nursery or primary school or a specialist unit you can visit for ideas. Contact The National Autistic Society, which will be able to send information about courses, useful publications and sources of support in your area.

Find out whether it is possible to give Yusef more support at nursery. You will need to assess whether or not his pushing behaviour will put other children at risk of being injured and if you need to provide additional support.

Many schools now have symbols programs on their computers. If you have access to one, print off symbols for some of the main classroom areas and activities. Label each main area of the classroom with a large symbol (about seven by seven centimetres in size). If you cannot find a symbols program, refer to the resources section at the back of this book, for ideas on where to find free symbols.

Think about where you could situate a quiet work area for Yusef. Preferably, this would be in the classroom, although, if he is very easily distracted, he may need to have a workspace outside the classroom to begin with.

Make up a timetable showing inside play, outside play and work. Place the drawings on a strip of card with Velcro. At first, show Yusef how to match the symbols with the large versions of the symbols in the respective areas. The large 'inside play' symbol can be placed somewhere uncluttered near his favourite activities. The 'outside play' symbol can be on the door to the outside play area. Increase the number of symbols you put on the timetable slowly. Too much information at once will be confusing and it may take several weeks for Yusef to understand what the symbols mean.

Find some noisy cause and effect toys that will interest Yusef immediately and some toys to use as rewards, such as bubbles, puzzles and musical toys.

Decide on consistent strategies to use to teach Yusef not to push other children. These would include teaching him to 'Wait' and to take turns with his peers, to develop an awareness of others and to slow down in the playground.

Write up an individual education plan for Yusef. Give him three or four short-term targets based on the information you have and the extra resources you can use. It may contain the following targets.

Baseline: *Yusef will sit briefly to begin activities he enjoys but does not remain seated.*

Target: *Yusef will sit down when asked to do so and complete a short play activity with adult support.*

Strategy:
> put out a short activity that Yusef enjoys which has a clear completion point, such as a puzzle or a posting toy
> tell him to sit down; praise him for 'good sitting'
> prompt him to stay sitting until he has finished his puzzle or do half the puzzle for him so he can finish it quickly, and if he gets up, bring him back to his seat
> when he has finished, praise him and stress that he has finished, saying, for example, 'Finished, clever boy!'
> repeat this several times throughout the morning using different activities
> gradually increase the length of time the activity will take.

Baseline: *Yusef rarely looks up when his name is called.*

Target: *Yusef will look towards an adult when his name is called.*

Strategy:
> call Yusef by name, maybe using a noisy toy to gain his attention and reward him immediately when he looks at you
> use motivating rewards, such as bubbles, spinning tops, noisy puppets.

Baseline: *Yusef plays on his own and ignores others around him.*

Target: *Yusef will play interactive games with an adult.*

Strategy:

> sit alongside Yusef and join in with what he is doing
> turn it into a turn-taking, interactive game
> sing about or copy what he is doing
> when Yusef enjoys the game, encourage another child to join in.

Baseline: *Yusef manipulates toys but does not use them for pretend play. For example, he will play with the wheels of a car but will not push the car along the ground. He prefers to play alone.*

Target: *Yusef will allow an adult to join in his play activities.*

Strategy:

> have an adult join Yusef when he is playing with a toy or activity he enjoys
> try having two sets of the same toys, if Yusef doesn't like to share
> make the play activity a lot of fun for Yusef and follow his lead and interests
> extend the play slowly to include different activities
> when it is going well, you could introduce turn-taking with an adult
> if that goes well you could introduce another child to the play activity.

It is unlikely that Yusef will be able to sit on the carpet with the rest of the group, although he may do so with adult help. If he finds nursery very hard and his behaviour is difficult to manage, then set up a structured work session for him straight away and build up the time he is working with an adult in his own work space. However, if he copes well with playing and learning new skills alongside his peers, then structured work will not be necessary at this stage.

It is important that all the adults in the nursery work with Yusef from the beginning and are not put off by his 'leave me alone' attitude. It is easy to unintentionally create a situation in which he builds a relationship with just one adult. Other adults need to play with Yusef as well and use any brief opportunity that arises to develop his interactive skills.

See Chapter 1 (page 13) for play suggestions.

Suggested structured or table-top activities for Yusef

Start by assessing what Yusef can do, then move him on to the next stage. When showing Yusef new skills:

> use consistent short instructions
> use modelling, prompting, forward and backward chaining.

When Yusef has mastered a skill, generalise what he has learnt to other activities in the nursery.

Here are some ideas for structured or table-top activities for Yusef.

> **Sorting objects**. Prepare a number of small objects to be sorted into pots – for example, clothes pegs, crayons, beads, bottle tops and feathers. Start with two or three different objects: five clothes pegs, five beads, five feathers and three pots to sort them into. Show him what to do using modelling and physical prompting. When Yusef can sort three different objects, increase the number.

> **Sorting objects by colour**. Lay out a red, blue, green and yellow bowl and a number of small, coloured objects to sort into the bowls. Alternatively, use a pegboard with large pegs and model how you want the pegs to be sorted. Using mosaic patterns is also good; the pegs are laid out according to a pattern underneath. However, this does require more skill.

> **Matching real objects to photos, line drawings, symbols or silhouettes**. Start with two drawings and two objects, then build up to ten.

> **Matching pictures to pictures**. It is easiest to do this using a lotto board with four clear pictures and matching cards or a board with strips of Velcro showing clearly where the pictures should be matched.

> **Match objects to shapes**. Use different sizes of bottle tops and a board with the shapes drawn onto one side in order of size, and on the other side at random.

> **Introduce new inset puzzles, form boards (puzzles in which common shapes need to be fitted into the right hole), posting boxes and simple four- to six-piece jigsaw puzzles.**

> **Build a construction following simple visual instructions**. Draw each step on a separate card and tie the cards together. Match the pieces to the ones on the card and add the next piece. Start with three simple pieces.

> **Thread fat beads or cotton reels on to a lace or piece of dowel**. Start with five beads.

> **Screw and unscrew lids**. You could put interesting items in screw-top pots, for example: a little coloured glitter, balloons or sequins.

> **Introduce a number of different drawing implements**.

> **Cut and stick**. Start with fringing or cutting thin strips of coloured or shiny paper.

> **Introduce new books**. Start with noisy or tactile books and lift the flap books.

It may take some time for Yusef to settle at nursery or at school and for staff to feel they have a relationship with him. If he finds the nursery environment overwhelming, and there are no adults available to support him, you may want to consider asking a family member to stay with him for some of the time, gradually decreasing in small steps as Yusef becomes more confident. If that is not possible, it may be necessary to introduce Yusef slowly to nursery, and build up the time he spends there from five to ten minutes a day to a whole session.

A structured, step-by-step approach reduces anxiety in a child with autism and offers a means to succeed. It is predictable, it includes tangible rewards, and it encourages the use of techniques and strategies that are positive and successful for the child. In the long term, it provides an anchor during the day that helps a child with autism tackle new challenges and deal with more difficult aspects of his day.

4. Developing literacy skills

Some children with autism will develop literacy skills quite easily and others will struggle. The range and type of difficulties they have will vary from small specific problems, to an inability to read or write at all. However, with support, a lot can be done to develop an interest in literacy. For preverbal children, the ability to read pictures and symbols can help enormously with speaking and listening.

Children are all taught to read using phonics but children with autism may need a little more groundwork than that. They can learn alongside their peers that letters have sounds, but because they are more rigid in their thinking, they can have problems understanding that the sounds combine to make a word, and that the written word has a meaning apart from 'c-a-t', for example.

Many of the ideas given below will be easier to do if your child has extra help for literacy, but they can be adapted quickly and will also benefit other children in the class. Fun activities in small bursts at home will also help a lot.

This chapter is divided into the following parts:

> developing an interest in books
> teaching a child with autism to read
> helping children with handwriting difficulties.

Developing an interest in books

Young children with autism spectrum disorders have difficulty seeing life from somebody else's perspective, so they often prefer non-fiction books, or stories that are very familiar and predictable. This does not mean they never show creativity, or the ability to make stories up, but they may need more support to understand the subtleties of some stories, or to understand which stories are made up and which are real-life. Books of all kinds – home-made books, journals, photos, schedule books and story books – are all essential because they have so many functions. Not only in reading stories, but in learning about the world, developing communication skills, helping with social understanding, reflecting on past experiences and so on.

Children sometimes become attached to certain books or catalogues and refuse to look at other books, or find it difficult to share a book or follow the language used in a story. If you are working with a child who is only interested in certain books such as catalogues or books with numbers and letters, these make a good starting point for developing early literacy skills.

You could use photographs of familiar people or pictures cut from catalogues to make books that will interest the child. They could be quite small books and it could be an enjoyable activity to make the book together. When looking for a book to share, choose books with clear, bright pictures that you think your child might enjoy. If they are linked to his special interests, try to expand the field as much as possible. An interest in Postman Pat, for example, can be extended to books about postmen, cats, vans or other television characters.

Books with noises or flaps are good for young children and tactile books are sometimes popular and certainly easy to make if you have time. Remember, though, that some children with autism spectrum disorders are sensitive to certain textures, although there may be others they particularly enjoy. The best advice is to be observant and to try different things.

For a young child with delayed communication skills, it is important to choose repetitive, simple stories and keep language at a level he can understand. At first, you may struggle to get through the book, turning one page at a time, but choose a book you can explore fully by lifting flaps, feeling textures and pressing buttons to make sounds. Point to pictures that might be familiar (cat, meow!) and gently prompt the child to point to the picture or say a sound or word. It should be a fun exploration rather than reading a story straight through.

Book bags or stories with props are helpful for all young children but particularly for those who have difficulty understanding the language and concept of a story. Stories can be prepared in advance and used daily until the child is ready to move on to another book. For example, a story about animals may come with assorted toy animals; the child learns to associate the pictures and the story with the animal by matching the correct animal to the picture in the book, the spoken word and the sound the animal makes. If you have a child who is particularly interested in animals, this can be extended to introduce a wide range of interesting information about food, babies, habitats and so on.

For a child who is learning that written words have meaning, the book bag activity can be extended so that the child matches the written word to the toy or prop and the picture in the book. If you have time to make books, copy the book, bind and laminate it and attach the words with Velcro. You could also attach a symbol or simplified drawing of the main picture on the page.

You could have a magnet board using pictures from the book to tell the story, making the pictures big and bright. When your child starts to recognise written words, he can match the words with the pictures on the board. This can also be a good group activity with children taking turns to choose the correct word or symbol.

It is important when looking at a storybook together to keep language simple and not to start reading a story with complex sentences to a child who does not have the language skills to understand.

Group stories can be made more accessible to children with language difficulties by using props, puppets and large pictures. To include a child with autism in a group story, give him a toy, a sound or a choice he can make linked to the story. For example, if you have a picture for each page, children in the class can take turns coming up and choosing the correct picture for that page or clicking or tapping their choice on the smart board.

Books of photographs with a single word or a short sentence describing each picture, as well as storybooks about children, families and familiar communities, can be more meaningful to children with an autism spectrum disorder than books in which animals dress in clothes, drive cars and talk to each other. The latter can be difficult for some children to understand, although they will enjoy them if they have seen the characters in a DVD or film.

Books about characters the child particularly likes will be motivating but may need to be rewritten or retold in simple language. You could use the characters to make books to help a particular child read and enjoy stories. It is often possible to find suitable pictures online that can be cut and stuck together to make suitable books. Or, simply tell the story in language that is accessible and fun.

Roleplaying simple stories can be an exciting activity for all children, and one that can include all levels of ability. Children love wearing simple costumes and enjoy repeating the same story with predictable lines and actions. They can wear masks they have made and decorated and join in with enthusiasm. Traditional stories like *The Three Little Pigs*, *The Big Turnip* and *The Gingerbread Man* are always popular for acting a part, using funny sounds and plenty of actions.

Children with autism spectrum disorders who can read may do so without understanding what they are reading. You can help them understand that stories have meaning and are not just a series of words on a page by making books using photographs of themselves and their family or friends. Spend time each day talking about familiar scenes in pictures and photographs before moving on to short picture books depicting everyday situations.

Teaching children with autism spectrum disorders to read

Some children with autism spectrum disorders learn to sight-read easily. They do not understand the sounds the different letters and groups of letters make, but seem to have a precocious skill in knowing what the words are. This skill is called hyperlexia. If a child has hyperlexia, everyone will be impressed by his ability when other children are struggling to learn to read. However, it is important to help a child with an autism spectrum disorder understand what he is reading. He needs to be aware of the content and plot of the story and the meanings of different words and concepts. Sometimes a child will read a text perfectly and retell the story by rote right through to the end, but will be unable to answer specific questions about the story because the meaning of the story has bypassed them. Giving choices and retelling the story in a different settling, or with different characters, can help when this is an issue.

Other children with autism have more difficulty learning to read. They may easily learn by rote the names and sounds of letters but be unable to understand that the sounds fit together to form a word. When they see a letter on the page, that is what they see; a letter name and a letter sound. They may appear to be learning to read because they know some storybooks off by heart, but then they fail to progress. They need a lot of help to understand that words have meanings and to see the whole word, not just the letters they have learnt.

In cases like these, it can be easier to use a multisensory approach and very motivating materials.

Words will be given meaning when they are attached to something that is meaningful to the child. You can start developing early reading skills by labelling items in the environment with a symbol or simple line drawing, and a word. At home you could label the fridge, television, computer and different rooms. At school, many things are routinely labelled but make sure labels are attached to items of particular interest to the child – the computer or headphones, for example. Then, when he is making choices, he can choose from a board of symbols and pictures, and later from two or more words. A first reading book can be made showing photographs of him at school using the things he enjoys.

At the simplest level, you can make up a book of photographs of family members or favourite foods and help your child match the appropriate word, name or symbol with each photograph. Using Velcro, so he can stick the words under the pictures, can make this activity more interesting, although there is also software available that will enable you to develop drag-and-drop boxes or simple touch-screen images. Any computer programme that teaches these early skills will be motivating, but real books are also important, so children generalise the skills they are learning to a range of media and situations.

If a child knows some books off by heart, photocopy the pictures, cut up the sentences and ask him to stick the sentences back in order and read them back to you. At first, this may be a simple matching exercise, finding the correct words and sticking them under the sentence, but, as the activity becomes more familiar, leave some gaps in the sentences so the child can fill the words in without the visual prompt. As a stepping stone to this activity you can also match symbols and words if you have the software that enables you to do this. Over time, the symbols can be made smaller and the word larger, until just the words are in use.

At the zoo
Fill in the missing letters on all the words

_lephant   _nake   _orilla

_ion   _angeroo   _eer

_ippo   _ear   _onkey

_amel   _iger   _iraffe

K, G, T, H, C, M, D, B, G, L, S, E

Teach whole words, starting with familiar names, words in the environment and words in books the child already knows. It sometimes helps to make up cards with the word and symbol on one side and the word alone on the other. It is then more likely that the child will always be successful, which is very motivating.

Remind the child to look at the page and try to guess from the picture what a word may be. Because children with autism have difficulty doing two things at once and making a connection between them, they do not usually think about the picture when they are trying to read a sentence. They need to be prompted to do so.

Rewrite simple storybooks using a symbols computer program so the child has the symbols to help. As most children with autism are visual learners who 'think in pictures', this can give them confidence and help give meaning to the words. As the child gains confidence, you can start leaving some symbols off words that are repeated a lot or can be easily guessed from the context.

When a child can read some words and is gaining confidence, work on initial letter sounds and then move on to more complex phonics. Using computer programs with pictures and symbols is a good way to teach initial sounds and has the added advantage of helping develop independent working skills.

Help children to make their own books. Use computer graphics, photographs, pictures, drawings or concrete reminders of trips out and special activities. Encourage the child to talk about what is on the page and write for him if necessary. Use his own words, even if it is only one word. You can always put a longer sentence underneath.

Reading and writing require sequencing skills. Many children with autism spectrum disorders have difficulty sequencing. Very early skills can be taught by sequencing patterns – for example, building a tower or threading beads following a coloured sequencing guide. At first, the child matches the beads to the guide and threads them. Then, as he becomes more confident, he may have ten beads but the guide shows the pattern for eight beads, then six, then four until he is able to continue a pattern of three or four beads. It is possible to buy books with a variety of different picture sequences to arrange in order, using cutting and sticking or putting a ring around the next picture in the sequence.

Sequencing language activities can be practised by using sets of sequencing cards, retelling events and stories in the correct sequence, understanding phrases such as 'What happened before?' and 'What happened next?' Use photos of the child doing an activity – making a fruit salad or getting dressed, say – and sequence them to make a book. Take it step-by-step.

Helping children with handwriting difficulties

Children with autism spectrum disorders often have difficulties with fine motor skills. They may not have enough control to hold the pencil and form a letter. Writing requires the physical skill of holding a pencil and forming a letter and the understanding that what they are doing has meaning. Either of these skills may be difficult for a child with autism. They may have sensory difficulties that affect the amount of control they have when manipulating their pencil. They may find it easier if you just put a little pressure on the top of their wrist while they are writing. If that is effective, there are special weighted bracelets children can wear round their wrists that help them control their pencil.

Sometimes they learn to form some capital letters that are easy, such as 'A' or 'O', and learn that that letter has a name. They receive a lot of praise from parents and teachers as they have begun to master an important skill. Then they copy the letter over and over and it is difficult to move them on.

Alternatively, they may learn to write numbers and then cover a piece of paper with numbers and nothing else. It can be hard to move a child forward when writing the same thing becomes fixed and repetitive. A lack of imagination may mean the child does not understand that the graphics they are using have meaning and represent objects.

What you can do

Teaching pre-writing skills

Teach hand-eye co-ordination by:
> playing skittles
> throwing a ball in a hoop
> doing lacing and threading activities
> tracing with a finger in damp or dry sand
> tracing along a line with paint on a finger
> tracing a simple picture outline with paint on a finger
> tracing over tactile letters and numbers (made from card, sand, glue or sandpaper stuck onto card)
> tracing shapes on each other's backs.

Help to strengthen hands by:
> squeezing a sponge during water play
> manipulating playdough or clay (squeeze, squash, roll and cut)
> banging on a drum or a hammer toy
> cutting and pasting – start with fringing paper then move on to cutting straight lines
> using tongs or tweezers to move objects from one container to another.

Improve hand manipulation by:

> screwing up little balls of paper and pasting them inside a shape to make a picture
> building using Lego and other construction toys
> taking lids off and putting lids onto bottles and jars
> opening other containers such as lunch boxes
> manipulating all kinds of fastenings: zips, big and small buttons or Velcro
> doing puzzles or placing pegs on pegboards.

Improve finger manipulation by:

> popping bubbles in the air
> doing finger painting
> using computer keyboards or telephones
> playing with switches.

Teach grasp and release by:

> picking up small objects
> popping bubble wrap
> holding pencils, pens, paintbrushes, crayons, chalk and making marks
> holding small objects like beads
> holding blocks and cubes, building towers or a marble run
> modelling with junk eg boxes, tubes.

Pencil skills

Start with early pencil skills. Can the child copy a straight line (horizontal, then vertical) or a circle? Can he draw a face or a person? Teach him to copy first a horizontal line, then a vertical line, a diagonal line then a circle. Use a physical prompt if necessary or share a large sheet of paper.

When the child is happy and confident using a pencil, show him how to hold it properly. It is important to do this because it could be difficult to alter how the child writes in future if you do not start him on the right track when he is young. Here are some ideas.

> Use large sheets of paper and write on them with highlighter pen, creating thick lines which the child can then trace over.

> Use a whiteboard, a flip chart or draw with chalk on a wall or on the ground.

> If the child holds his pen loosely and makes light marks that are difficult to see, give him fat, brightly coloured pens. There may be sensory issues that affect the way he feels the pen in his hand, or his perception of how hard he needs to press to make marks on the paper.

> Make cards of patterns for the child to trace over. Laminate them so he can write directly on the cards and you can wipe them clean. Use lines, simple shapes and spirals, depending on the ability of the child.

> Drawing half a face or half a shape that the child has to finish is good for developing pencil skills. You can start by drawing half on a large sheet of paper and show the child how to copy on his side of the paper. When he has the idea, you can make up laminated cards for him to finish.

> Use a writing scheme that teaches how to form letters in groups that have similar shapes, for example, a, c, d, g, o, q, s and b, f, h, k and p.

Capitals and lower case

Children are sometimes taught to write in capitals at home. This may seem sensible because capitals are easier to form and children learn them more quickly. However, it is very difficult to teach a child to use lower-case letters once they have learnt to use capitals and writing in capitals is very slow. Generally, it is better not to teach a child to use capitals unless every other strategy has failed.

Cursive writing

Because some children with autism spectrum disorders have such difficulty learning to write and dislike changing their technique, it may be worth considering teaching cursive (joined-up) writing from the beginning.

Lines

Many children with autism spectrum disorders need lines as a guide when they are writing. They have difficulty creating their own imaginary lines and sometimes their writing just gets larger and larger.

Writing independently

Children may learn to trace or copy but have difficulty writing independently. When a child has learned to trace over his name confidently, leave off the last letter. If he does not fill it in, leave off the end of the last letter. Each time he writes his name leave off a little bit more. If necessary prompt him to complete his name, but try to do it lightly and withdraw the prompt next time.

Developing understanding of words

Teach words that are meaningful to the child. Children with autism will sit and copy over letters with no understanding of their meaning. They may find it hard to transfer the skill of forming letters along a line in a book to writing words that have meaning.

Teach words they can read that are linked to their interests. If a child wants you to write out the names of every tube station on the Northern Line, do it, then after several days of writing them leave off the last letter of the last station and ask him to complete it. He may be upset but you can give a gentle prompt by placing your hand on his wrist and he may discover he can do it. Gradually expect him to do more writing, it will develop his confidence and it will become easier to find other ways of encouraging independent writing.

Overcoming fear of failure

Children with autism spectrum disorders can become anxious about making mistakes. This sometimes prevents them doing any work unless they feel confident they can do it perfectly.

A Social Story™ (see Chapter 6, page 114) can be helpful to reassure them that it is okay to make mistakes. You may find it easier to let them use an eraser initially, then gradually limit when they can use it. Maybe you could let them use it for tasks they will find difficult, but not for routine tasks.

Reference material

Children sometimes find it easier to write independently if they can see the alphabet on their book or table. They then have a visual reminder of what the letters look like.

Keyboard skills

Teach keyboard skills to children with autism who have writing difficulties. Make sure right from the beginning that they use both hands. They may start off by typing with two fingers but they should use their left and right hands for the left and right sides of the keyboard. There are many typing programs available for children that are a lot of fun.

Whatever difficulties a child with autism may have when developing his literacy skills, a consistent approach that combines repetition with creative use of the child's special interests to develop teaching materials is a good starting point. As the child gains confidence, new topics can be introduced, providing they follow small steps and do not demand too big a leap in understanding. It may seem at first that you have to spend a lot of time adapting materials for one child. However, you will find with practice that you can develop new materials quickly and there may be other children who can also benefit from your expertise.

5. Teaching an understanding of number

Children with autism spectrum disorders are often very good at reciting and ordering numbers. Many recognise written numbers from one to ten at an early age and love to name them and line them up. They find it easy to learn by rote and may learn to count to large numbers but not understand a simple instruction like 'Give me two pencils', even when the instruction is given with a visual number two.

In order to move on and learn to use maths in daily routines, a child needs to have a firm grasp of basic number concepts. Real understanding of number may only come after a lot of practice of repetitive, practical activities.

What you can do

There are many opportunities throughout the day at home and school to teach an understanding of number. For example, counting eyes, ears, buttons on coats, steps, jumps, bounces of ball, spoons, plates, biscuits, sweets, grapes, apples and so on. Although new concepts and structured activities are best taught at a quiet time when there are few distractions, number skills the child has learned should be supported by plenty of practical examples at home and school.

Matching

In the early stages, it can be helpful to have cards, each showing a number and with spaces drawn at the bottom as a simple matching exercise. The child then matches small objects to the spaces.

There are many wonderful resources to help children develop early number concepts but sometimes children with autism find the colours and quantity of objects overwhelming rather than meaningful. Similarly, many children learn and practise skills through play, but a child with autism will need guidance and prompting in order to do so. Simple information, clearly and visually presented with plenty of practical experience to support it, is best at this stage.

For example, you may be working on understanding the numbers one and two. Make up number cards showing the numbers one and two – you will need these later. Now, make bigger cards showing the numbers one and two with circles or squares underneath or a strip of Velcro. The child can then either match an object to the circles or squares or stick one or two pictures onto the Velcro.

When a child can match the correct number of objects to the number on each card, use the smaller cards you made earlier without the squares. Hold one up, then ask the child to drop the matching number of objects into a posting box (empty crisps tubes are good as they make a satisfying 'clunk' when the object drops in). You could then thread the right number of beads or cotton reels on to a lace, put biscuits on to a plate, drop balls down the helter-skelter or do whatever other similar activity you choose.

When you have had plenty of practice with one and two, increase the numbers gradually to five, then to ten.

Using PECS can be a good way to teach number. If a child is asking for a piece of apple, he will quickly learn that asking for two pieces is better than asking for one.

Number songs

You can use number songs alongside pictures that are stuck to a board, and added and counted as each verse is sung. Many number songs introduce numbers in diminishing order. It is best to adapt these songs and start at number one, increasing to number five.

For example, if you have 15 yellow ducks and a magnetic board you could sing *Five little ducks*.

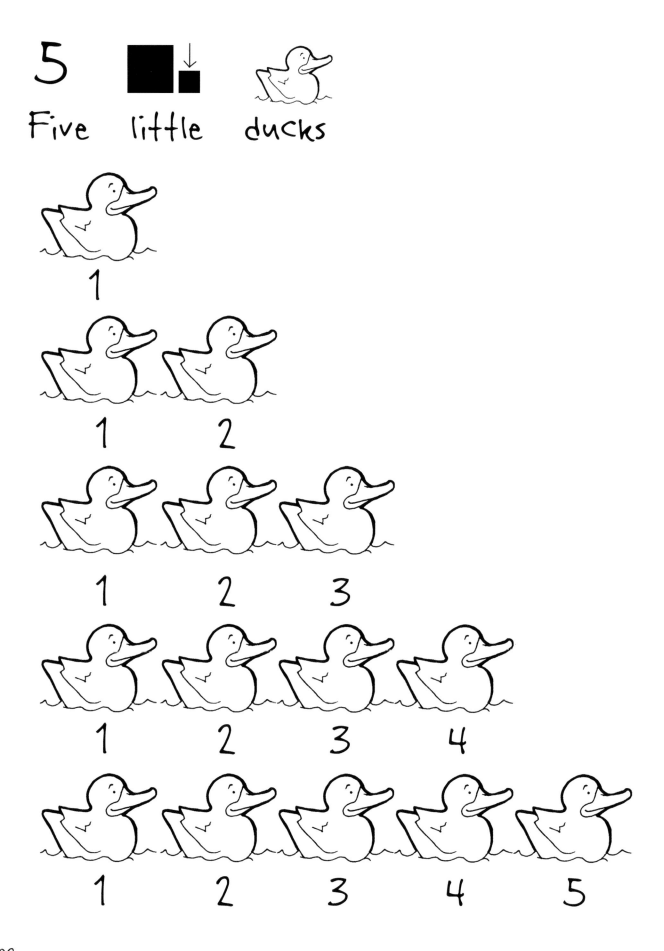

5　■▪↓　🦆

Five　little　ducks

Five little ducks

Five little ducks went swimming one day,
Over the hill and far away,
Mother duck said 'Quack, quack, quack',
But only one little duck came back.
(child puts one duck on the board)

Five little ducks went swimming one day,
Over the hill and far away,
Mother duck said 'Quack, quack, quack',
But only two little ducks came back
(child puts two ducks on the board)

... and so on to five.

Songs like this can be varied in many different ways. If you are teaching 'add one', the child can put one duck on the board each time and count the total as he goes. If you are teaching 'take away one', the child can start with five ducks on the board and take one off each time, counting how many ducks are left.

Activity books

You could make an activity book using laminated pages, with picture and number cards attached using Velcro. The ducks can then be removed and counted, added or subtracted on each page, depending what you are working on at the time.

If a child has special interests, you may be able to use that to help develop an understanding of number. If he likes trains, for example, you could do some work with trains, carriages, signals, drivers and so on. You could make a number line with a train and numbered carriages or make a book and ask him to put a certain number of people in each carriage. If you have access to a digital camera, you could make the book more interesting by using photos of family members or other children in the class. If you do make a book and you want the child to match a number on each page with a number of objects or people, it can be helpful to put all the numbers and all the pictures on Velcro. Then, when the child has learnt the numbers in order, you can jumble them up and teach them in a different order.

Chapter 5: Teaching an understanding of number

Using computers

There are also many apps for computers that teach the meaning of number and you may find your child grasps the concept very quickly when it is on a game with a visual and auditory reward. However, remember to generalise what he has learnt on the computer to real situations, examples he can hold and feel, as well as pen and paper activities.

Increasing understanding

When a child has counted a number of objects arranged in a line (for example, small cubes), jumble them up and ask him to count them again while they are spread out on the table. Many children with autism spectrum disorders have difficulty doing this and it can help them to provide a pot or tub to count the objects into.

Stamping activities

Stamps and a stamp pad can be good fun to use for counting activities.

You can give a child a piece of paper with a number on it and ask him, for example, to 'stamp four cats'. When he has more understanding and can work independently, he can go down a page of numbers, stamping the correct number of pictures beside each one.

As a variation, draw or cut and stick the correct number of objects beside each number. Link the pictures used to favourite stories or interests.

Using dice

Play dice games so the child learns to recognise numbers up to six without counting the dots each time.

One easy game to play uses a dice, counters and a board of squares for each player. The child throws the dice and covers the correct number of squares with counters. The first person to cover all their squares is the winner. Some children may need to practise with an adult first, but, when they are confident, ask another child to play too.

Beginning to add

Many children with autism spectrum disorders can count up to ten but become confused when shown how to add and, in particular, how to use a number line. One reason for this may be that they have not developed a concept of number and need to practise some of the ideas given above. When you are sure the child does have some concept of number, you can practise adding on.

Start adding on using practical examples. Do not introduce paper and pencil until you are sure the child is ready. Looking at numbers and writing an answer is an additional skill, so give a good grounding using practical examples first. After counting a set of objects, ask the child what the total would be if he added 'one more'.

Use the same phrase until you are sure the child understands it. Then introduce new vocabulary gradually. Children with autism are inflexible in their thinking and have difficulty generalising what they have learnt from one example to another. Every time they learn a new way to do the same thing, it can be like starting again, so take it slowly, step by step, and use plenty of visual examples.

> Use your fingers and ask the child to count how many fingers you are holding up.

> Use large die with dots. Throw two die and ask the child to count the number of dots on the tops of the die. If he recognises the number of dots on one dice he can count on from that number. Alternatively, use one dice with numbers and one with dots. Throw them both and ask the child to count on from the number dice. Similarly, you can use dominoes instead of die.

> Before introducing a number line, teach the child to count on using a simple game board with ten blank squares and a large dice with numbers on the faces. Two children could play if they both have their own board.

When the child is confident counting along the squares, number the squares and use two die with dots totalling no more than ten. The child counts the dots on the first dice, finds that number and puts his counter on it. He then counts the number on the second dice and counts on. You can put an additional Velcro strip at the bottom of the board and a set of numbers so the child can see the corresponding number at each stage of the process. When he is confident with this, try introducing a number line.

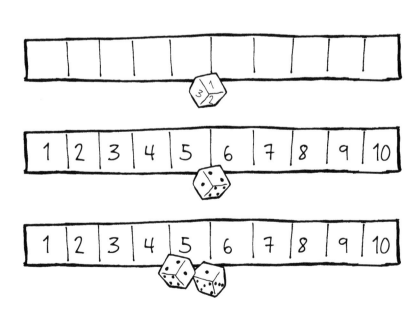

Some children are very good at mental maths. For those who find it difficult, teach them a visual strategy. Put your hand on your head to remember the number. If they still have difficulty, using fingers to aid early adding and subtracting can be more positive than not succeeding at all. Using fingers to add can also help children who struggle with maths and are very dependent on using small cubes – they have the added advantages of always being available and portable!

When you introduce mathematical concepts such as 'more', 'less', 'all', 'some', 'before' and 'after' remember that these concepts can be difficult to grasp for children with language difficulties. Symbols are available that depict these abstract number concepts and their consistent use can support understanding, as can all forms of visuals, using everyday, familiar opportunities, for example, cooking and shopping, playing with cars, building towers and playing interactive games on the computer.

6. Developing social skills

Children with autism spectrum disorders have difficulty understanding and interacting with others. They may be aloof or eccentric, run around with the other children in the playground but not interact with them, be confused by social overtures and have difficulty expressing themselves. Children who have sensory difficulties will also find the noise, movement and proximity of others in the playground and classroom hard to cope with.

What you can do

Learning to share

With young children in a nursery, you need to set up situations where the child learns to share and take turns. Turn-taking activities have been covered more fully in Chapter 1 (page 29) as it is also important in developing early communication and play skills.

Start by playing games in which you take turns. Say 'My turn' then 'Your turn'. When your child accepts taking turns with an adult, invite another child to join in. Say 'My turn, your turn, Johnnie's turn.'

In this way, children learn to understand their turn will come and the toy they want so much has not gone forever.

Teach the child to 'wait'

This is an important social skill that helps a child to take turns and share without becoming distressed. For more on this subject, see Chapter 2 (page 57).

Model play skills

Model a play routine that the child enjoys and when he is confident playing with an adult or older sibling, invite one or two other children to join in.

Awareness of others

If a child walks over other children on the carpet without realising that they are there, try giving him his own place to sit on the carpet. Make this spot near the edge so he can get out easily.

Also, show him how to step over other children. If his language skills are good, teach him to say 'Excuse me' and write a Social Story™ with photographs about saying 'Excuse me.'

Social interaction tasks

Teach children with autism how to do tasks that involve social interaction. For example, show a child how to go to the office with a sensible classmate to get the register, give out milk or fruit, choose a story for the whole class from a choice of two or three at story time, and so on.

If you have times when you sing in the nursery, have a picture for each song pinned to a board and invite the children to choose one. If you are telling a story to a group of children, include an element of choice or an action that a child with autism can do to join in.

Buddies

Implementing a buddy system for the playground can be very beneficial.

Buddies can be children as young as four or five, providing they are told what to do and when to get adult help. However, they can also be chosen from older classes. Buddies wear buddy badges or bright baseball caps and feel special for the day. It is important to ask for volunteers to be a buddy every day otherwise it may fall too much to one or two children.

Buddy badge

A buddy system can also be reassuring for parents who may be worried that their child will be bullied in a large playground.

If two buddies are chosen every day, they find it easier than an adult to stay with one child as he moves around the playground and it is much better for a child to be supported by his peers than always by an adult.

Discuss social matters

Talk to all the children about helping each other. Young children may be egocentric but they can understand why some children need extra support. There are some nice books available for young children that tackle the issues of disability and inclusion, such as *My friend Sam* (see resources on page 152).

Utilise classroom assistants

If a child has adult support, use that person to enable him to join in group activities. It is easy to create a situation in which a child who has support is interacting all the time with an adult separate from the rest of the class. It is also important right from the start that all adults in a class or nursery interact with all the children, including those who have additional needs.

Make the most of circle time

Use circle time to encourage children to take turns and listen to others.

You can make this explicit by having an object that each child holds when it is his or her turn to speak. This can be developed further in a small group by checking that the children are listening to each other. You could do this subtly by pretending that you did not hear and ask the child holding the object what the previous child said.

Set up a lunchtime club

The club can make organised games and activities available so that children who need extra help with social interaction and play skills can have support. Each child can invite a friend and it can be a special time to teach new social and play skills.

Lunchtime clubs can also focus on children's special interests, maybe once a week. Younger children could have a Thomas the Tank Engine club or a dinosaur club and older children could have a computer club. Whatever the subject, it is an opportunity for the child with autism to be with others who share his interests and hobbies.

Games and other play activities

Try to set up situations in which children have to play together in pairs or small groups to complete a game or activity. There are many suggestions for turn-taking games in Chapter 1 (page 29), and these can be developed into slightly more complex games as the child gets older. Traditional games like *Ring a ring o' roses*, skipping, and simple ball games provide a structure for young children who may be struggling with social interaction skills to join in games with their peers.

Circle of friends

'Circle of friends' is an idea that originated in the USA to help support the inclusion of children with additional educational needs in mainstream schools.

It is an effective technique that uses peer support to help children who are having difficulties with social interaction, independence skills and learning. It is most suitable for children in Key Stage Two and older, although a younger child could have a circle of friends if there was plenty of adult support available at the beginning.

A circle of friends is usually a group of eight children, with the focus child, supported by an adult. The group meets weekly for 20 to 30 minutes for the first ten weeks, then decides whether to carry on meeting as often.

The idea behind the circle of friends is that the child's peer group makes decisions and works out strategies that will help the key child find solutions to difficulties he may be having.

Example 1
Luke is a quiet Year three boy who has only recently been diagnosed with autism. He has always been to a mainstream school with additional adult support.

He has coped fairly well with a differentiated curriculum, but at playtime he was either on his own or played with much younger children. He recently started hitting out at other children on the stairs or at other unstructured times during the day but was not able to express his feelings, even to adults he knew well.

At his first annual review following his diagnosis of autism, the specialist teacher for children with autism spectrum disorders discussed the possibility of having a circle of friends with Luke's parents. They liked the idea and when it was discussed with Luke, he thought it sounded good and that it would help him.

The specialist teacher volunteered to come in to talk to the class and run the circle for ten weeks with the learning support assistant, who was able to feed back what had been happening during the week. During the class talk, Luke was taken out to the library to work.

The class was told what a circle of friends was for and how it would work. The pupils were encouraged to think about things they found difficult and how they would feel if they had difficulty making friends. They were then asked to think about the things that Luke was good at and a list was drawn up. A list was also drawn up of things he found difficult at school.

The teacher suggested that friends can help with things that are difficult and that a circle of friends could help Luke and make him feel happier. The children were told that they would have to give up one lunchtime play every week and were then asked to volunteer. Many more than eight children volunteered, so the teacher chose a group he felt would be most supportive. Everyone was reminded to support the circle of friends, even if they had not volunteered or been chosen.

All the parents' permission was sought and, once the permission slips were in, the circle began. It met one lunchtime a week and began by looking again at Luke's strengths and the things he found difficult – this time with him contributing.

Some things were targeted and strategies agreed on. In particular, the friends agreed to help Luke in the playground by teaching him games and making sure he was included.

The circle started off well, but by the fourth week it ran into difficulties. The two girls were finding that they had all the responsibility for supporting Luke at playtime and one girl dropped out. Her brother had autism and she found that playing a supporting role at school as well as at home was too much for her. The boys wanted to play football all the time and Luke was slow and clumsy, with minimal ball skills. Everyone, apart from Luke, felt that they did not want to give up a lunchtime play every week. They tried to disappear out of the classroom before the circle of friends meeting began. Only Luke was happy with the circle of friends. He felt he had friends and his self-esteem was growing week by week.

The learning support assistant and the teacher encouraged each child in the circle to say what was going well and what was going badly. They were asked to think of what they could do about the bad things and each child gave an opinion or made a suggestion. They decided to take turns every day to support Luke in the playground and to try some new games that other children might enjoy. They also decided to ask the teacher to speak to the class, reminding them to support the circle of friends and to find another girl to join the circle.

Two girls joined the circle and the rota system worked so well that, after a few weeks, it was tacitly dropped.

At the end of the ten weeks, the members of the circle were asked to say what they thought about how it had gone. They all felt positive about it and wanted it to continue. They suggested a posting box where they could write down things they needed to talk about with the learning support assistant or class teacher.

A year on, Luke is so much more confident that he seems a different boy. He is able to speak out in a stronger voice and give his opinion about things. He feels he has friends and knows where to turn when he is having difficulties or is unhappy.

A circle of friends rarely runs smoothly from beginning to end. However, sorting out difficulties in a structured group with adult support is a very positive experience for children. The important thing is that they work things through themselves and take credit for their success.

Theory of mind

In 1995, S. Baron-Cohen argued that one feature of autism spectrum disorders may be a failure of the individual to develop a 'Theory of Mind'. Research has shown that children with autism have great difficulty taking others' thoughts into account and may not even be aware that you have your own thoughts and needs. They may also believe you know what they are thinking, so they will start a conversation with no reference to what the conversation is about. They have difficulty showing empathy with others, expressing their own feelings or predicting from non-verbal cues or previous experience what will happen in a social situation. This sometimes results in finding others' behaviour confusing or frightening, causing anxiety, fear and sudden aggressive or unexpected behaviour.

What you can do

> Make your meaning clear and do not assume that a child with an autism spectrum disorder knows what you mean by your facial expression, gestures or tone of voice.

> Try to be calm and keep your voice calm in the classroom.

> If possible, give the child his own quiet corner where he can work if he is having difficulty coping in a group.

> Try different things that may be calming, such as listening to music through headphones.

> Organise the child's support so there is help at unstructured times of the day.

> Give him a routine activity at transition times so he knows exactly what to do.

> Use stories, photos, drawings and real situations to talk about feelings. Start with simple, familiar feelings, such as happy, sad, angry and scared.

> Use toys and puppets to model feelings or responses to feelings.

> If there is an incident in the playground, classroom or at home, draw pictures to help the child talk about it and how different individuals might be feeling.

Examples of symbols used to talk about feelings

Happy Sad Scared Angry

I got pushed

> Children who can read, but who find it hard to express their feelings might be able to do so if you write down what you say (or type it on a computer) and then write down their response without looking at them directly. They are then more focused on what you are saying and more able to follow the conversation because reading it on the page is easier than speaking, and they do not need to hold so much information in their heads. This is because visual information is easier for them to understand and interpret than auditory information even when it might seem that their language skills are good.

It can be difficult to help children with autism spectrum disorders to develop social understanding, but generally it is best to use real situations to explore meanings and emotions and to reflect on what has happened. If a child does have the communication skills to explain an event, (or a drawing of an event), from his own perspective, you may be surprised how his interpretation of what has happened differs from yours. You can learn a great deal from this and use it as a starting point to help the child become less confused in social situations.

For children who do not have the communication skills to discuss what went wrong, you can use photos, videos, drawings, modelling and shaping behaviour to develop understanding and teach a more correct response. You need to have a long-term view however, as understanding what went wrong in one situation will not always be generalised to others.

Social Stories™

Social Stories™ were developed in the USA by Carol Gray (see references, page 147). If they are constructed properly, they can work wonderfully for children who are having difficulties understanding social situations and managing to cope with change.

They work best for children who have the ability to understand simple sentences, but they can also be presented in pictures, symbols or with photographs to help younger or less able children understand what to do in certain social situations or to reassure them that what is happening is going to be okay.

For example, when children are moving up to reception from nursery, they could have a Social Story™ to prepare them for the change. The story could be in book form with photographs showing the new classroom, the new teacher and the things that will still be the same – the children, the learning support assistant, the work bay for individual work and so on.

Carol Gray describes the three main types of sentences that are to be found in her Social Stories™. These are:

> **descriptive**: describing what is happening or what will happen and why
> **perspective**: describing how people feel and react to certain situations
> **directive**: describing what should happen in a given situation.

For example:
When I go to dinner I line up with my class. (*descriptive*)
Miss Jones usually comes with me. (*descriptive*)
We walk to the dining hall. (*descriptive*)
Sometimes the dinner ladies are busy and we have to wait for our dinner. (*descriptive*)
This can make me worried so that I want to scream. (*perspective*)
I will try to look at my picture book, relax and wait quietly for dinner. (*directive*)
Then after dinner I will have ten minutes computer time and Miss Jones will be happy. (*descriptive*).

Carol Gray's stories use descriptive and perspective sentences. A short story will have one directive statement only. She uses phrases such as 'usually' and 'I will try to...' in order to avoid making statements that leave no room for error or exceptions. This is because children with autism spectrum disorders will often take what is said very literally and find it hard to accept changes to rules.

In the example given above, photos could be used to make a book with sentences, thought or speech bubbles, and symbols depicting emotions.

Carol Gray has edited books of Social Stories™ that are a good starting point if you want to start writing your own stories for particular children and situations. The stories can be adapted and give good examples of what to write and what works well.

Social Stories™ should not contain negative statements; they are factual and offer a positive outcome and a means of understanding why things happen.

Example 2

Jack was coping very well in his mainstream primary school and his literacy skills were developing well. However, he lacked the confidence to work independently because he was always worried that he would make an error and erasers were not allowed in the classroom.

Even when an exception was made for him, Jack could not relax because he knew that, by using an eraser, he was breaking a class rule.

Adults working with him decided to try a Social Story™, which he read before he started his written work and it was then placed where he could easily see it. This is what it said:

Sometimes when I am writing I make a mistake.
Sometimes other children in my class make mistakes.
Mrs Brown tells us to put a cross through the mistake.
I will try to put a cross through my mistakes and carry on with my work.
Mrs Brown will be pleased that I have finished my work by myself.
She will give me a special sticker when I cross out my mistakes and finish my work.

Within three weeks, Jack was able to do his writing and cross out his mistakes without anxiety.

7. Lack of imagination and flexible thought

Children with autism spectrum disorders have difficulty with imagination and flexible thinking. This will present itself in a number of different ways but in younger children it particularly affects the way they play. Young children learn through play and it is more difficult for them to learn and socialise with their peers if they do not play and are not able to think imaginatively and flexibly.

They also have difficulty generalising what they have learnt across a range of settings and become confused if a task or routine they know well is changed or presented in a different way.

They may have good language skills but take everything literally. When they are told to 'go and get in the bath', for example, they may do just that, but do not take off their clothes or run the water.

They are often resistant to change and can become very distressed if the daily routine changes or new displays are put up on the classroom walls.

The following examples are just some of the strategies that can be tried to help young children become more flexible and imaginative. However, although it is possible to teach play routines and help children to make choices and manage change, the inflexibility of a child with an autism spectrum disorder is a difficult aspect to alter. As is stressed throughout this book, it is important to be aware of the difficulties, teach skills in small steps using visual prompts, have clear targets and be creative when looking for solutions.

Example 1
John manipulates the wheels of a toy but does not play with it imaginatively.

Target: *John will extend his play with cars, trains and other toys, with adult support.*

Strategies you could try might include:
> teaching play skills by modelling what he can do with different toys
> if possible, having two identical toys and encouraging him to copy you
> using toys that capture his interest, such as noisy puppets, big sunglasses, floppy hats, squeaky teddies, cars with lights and sirens, balls with bells inside and so on

> teaching pretend play using the home corner, construction equipment, small world toys
> taking everything step by step and using a lot of repetition and prompting; making it really exciting and building on interests he shows in his play
> when he has learnt a play routine, inviting another child to join in
> if John enjoys watching videos, making a video of some children playing with a particular toy (cars on a car mat, train and train track or construction) and giving John the same toys to encourage him to copy.

Example 2
Josie does not play imaginative games with her peers but will play solitary games based on DVD or storybook characters.

Target: *Josie will join in a class game based on a story theme.*

Strategies you could try might include:
> using drama and group games to develop new ideas, for example, developing a theme over several days linked to a story or a particular topic
> having a clear target and working on it in small steps, such as 'Josie will pretend to be on a boat in a storm'
> using simple props – eye patches for pirates and large construction blocks for the boat with music, wind, rocking waves and other special effects, for example
> using modelling, prompting and repetition to show Josie what to do.

Example 3

Joshua insists that games are played in certain ways and becomes distressed if somebody tries to change them.

Target: *Joshua will accept other children joining in and changing the rules or storyline of his games.*

Strategies you could try might include:

> joining in the game and making very subtle changes at first by breaking it down into very small steps, such as:
>   • Joshua will allow an adult to take a turn with his fire engine
>   • Joshua will interact with an adult when playing with his fire engine
>   • Joshua will follow an adult's ideas and let her follow his when playing with his fire engine
>   • Joshua will allow another child to join him when he is playing with an adult
> persevering with this until Joshua accepts more flexibility with his game
> teaching Joshua new games in structured settings, then generalising them to classroom and playground settings
> using a Social Story™ to explain how children play games and adding Joshua's ideas.

Example 4

Jamie will be upset for the whole day if his routine is changed in any way.

Target: *Jamie will accept small changes to his daily routine without crying.*

Strategies you could try might include:

> writing a Social Story™ to prepare Jamie for changes in advance – for example, what will happen when his teacher is away
> preparing him for big changes, such as moving to a new class, by having a transition plan which might include a Social Story™ with photographs and visits to the new class
> using a timetable and changing it immediately if there are any alterations
> using a consistent substitute for a cancelled favourite activity (swimming, for example)
> trying to avoid unnecessary changes.

Example 5

George is obsessed with his collection of dinosaurs and does not want to put them down when he comes into the classroom. He writes about dinosaurs and always insists on having a dinosaur somewhere in all his drawings.

Target: *George will play with three dinosaurs when he has finished his work.*

Strategies you could try might include:

> implementing a rule that George is only allowed to bring three dinosaurs into class – this will be hard for his family, so gradually decrease the number of dinosaurs by allowing one less every week and helping George to understand this by showing it on a visual chart

> writing a Social Story™ telling George when he can have his dinosaurs or talk and write about them

> reducing anxiety for George at school by providing a structure with visual guidance

> using the dinosaurs as a reward for completing work and showing on his timetable when he is allowed to play, talk or write about them

> letting George have a special dinosaur project in which he has to find out broader things about dinosaurs, such as what the world was like then, how they looked after their babies and so on

> using dinosaurs to help George with things he finds difficult – adding and subtracting, classifying and sorting, for example (though these are not George's dinosaurs so, if he finds them distracting and inaccurate, use something else – you could even try using photos of his dinosaurs or clip art dinosaurs for adding activities and so on).

Example 6

Shereen has very good literacy skills but has difficulty writing about fictional characters or telling stories unless they are based on her favourite movie characters.

Target: *Shereen will retell simple stories that are not based on movie characters.*

Strategies you could try might include:

> using puppets, dressing-up items, simple props and role play to encourage imaginative play and new ideas

> sequencing photographs of something Shereen has done – for example, a role play, dressing-up game, day out, cooking or art activity, writing a caption for each page and making it into a book

> retelling a familiar story using the pictures in the book as a guide

> retelling a familiar story and asking Shereen to draw her own pictures to make a book

> talking about a single picture, about why something happened, what happened before and what might happen next and using drawings and speech bubbles to help plan out the story sequence

> building the single picture into a story by asking Shereen to draw before and after pictures and writing an accompanying story

> using other prompts such as objects, situations, other stories and so on.

Example 7

Michael takes language literally and will sometimes misunderstand what is said or feel threatened by it.

Target: *Michael will learn the meanings of common sayings and idioms.*

Strategies you could try might include:

> making sure adults working with Michael are aware of what they are saying and are checking that Michael has understood what has been said

> teaching the meaning of common ambiguous sayings, such as 'that was a tongue-twister', using drawings and discussion.

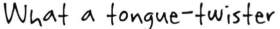

Coping with staff changes, moving classes, moving house and going on outings

All these major events can be traumatic for any child, but more so for a child who has autism who could have difficulty with:

> understanding and remembering verbal information about what is going to happen – he might understand your words but have a very different idea about what they mean to him

> grasping the sequence of events

> feeling anxious about losing structures and routines that make him feel safe

> feeling anxious about losing possessions or friends who are important

> coping with strange people and places

> being sensitive to sounds, movement, colours, lights, smells that are unfamiliar

> not knowing unspecified expectations (for example, how to behave with strangers).

Some children on the autism spectrum cope very well with change, or ignore major changes but react badly to small changes. However, until you are sure you have a child who doesn't mind change, you should have a plan to ease the way.

Sharing information between home and school

When you know you are moving house, tell your child's teacher in advance so she can help you prepare the way. If possible, take photos of the new house and write a Social Story™. The Social Story™ can be in the form of a small picture book that will reassure your child about what is going to happen, what order it will happen in, and what it will mean, for example, new route to school, different play-park. Include pages that show everything that is important (computer, toys or tv, for example) will still be there. Sometimes, children settle well in their new home but are upset at school so the teacher should be aware that things are changing.

Similarly, personal things that you may not want to talk about, like relationship problems, family members going away, expecting a baby or experiencing a bereavement should be shared with the teacher if it is affecting your child's behaviour. You don't need to go into details – the teacher won't judge you – and of course things will be confidential. But it can be a big help for the teacher who could be worried about why Tommy has suddenly started displaying anxious behaviour, or refusing to co-operate in the classroom.

Going on outings

Outings are fun and a great way to learn, but they can also be a cause of anxiety. If you are going on a day outing by public transport make a picture book and describe what will happen. Warn your child in advance that there might be changes if things go wrong. Carry a 'change' symbol with you on the day if you think it will be needed.

It can be helpful to download photos of where you are going and be specific about the buses you might catch, if the child in question notices these things. Have a general plan for the day and use phrases like 'we will try to…'. Some younger children will respond best to a schedule using simple symbols, photographs or drawings. You can take off a symbol as each event is finished. For example, a simple schedule might include walk, wait for bus, bus, walk, museum, packed lunch, museum, play park, walk, bus, school, home.

A more complex schedule might need to specify which buses you are waiting for, what will happen in the museum, whether lunch will be in a specific room and so on.

Change

Go to toilet

Coat on

Walk to bus stop

Wait for number 12 or 171 bus

Ride on bus

Walk to museum

Look inside museum

Eat packed lunch

Leave museum

Play park

Walk to bus stop

Wait for number 12 or 171 bus

Ride on bus

School

Home

Changing classes

You can prepare your child for class and staff changes by making a book of photos to take home over the summer holidays. Photos should include all key staff, and a reassurance of which special friends will be in the same class and which favourite activities will remain unchanged. Discuss beforehand with his new teacher whether he will still need a work station and whether he will have learning aids like computer tablets, relaxation breaks and so on. Make sure he has visited the classroom several times and had some opportunities to meet his teachers and support workers. If he is going to a different building and using different toilets, a different dining room or another playground then it can be a big help to use those facilities during the last two or three weeks of the school term.

Writing a personal profile or passport

In order to help children and staff with changes it can be helpful if children with autism or other disabilities have a 'passport' that goes with them to different adults and outlines key information about what they need in order to be able to keep calm and focus throughout the day. If you are working with a child who can contribute to his passport this is a great activity to do in preparation for moving up to another class. It can be simple or illustrated with drawings and photos.

Example: My Passport

About me:
> My name is Luc Smith.
> I am 6 years old. My birthday is 16 March.
> I live with my mum and dad. I have a baby sister called Issy.
> I come to school by taxi.

I am good at:
> computers
> making things with Lego
> reading.

I need help with:
> adding
> walking on the stairs
> finishing my work
> coming into class after playtime.

Things I like are:
> computer games (my favourite is Dora the Explorer)
> Lego, picture books (especially with animals), running.

I get anxious when:
> I have to come in after play
> I have changes to my routine
> I can't do my work.

Things that help are:
> using a timer, traffic lights cards
> using my schedule, relaxation
> regular work breaks, rewards.

My rewards are:
ten minutes on an iPad after each completed work session (three times a day).

8. Sensory issues

One other major area of difficulty that most people with autism have are sensory issues. These are mentioned briefly on page 10. However, they are so important that they need a little more explanation before we discuss behaviour support strategies.

People with autism may process sensory stimulation very differently to the way 'neurotypical' people do. We know this largely from the experiences of people with autism, who are the best source of information on the subject of autism spectrum disorders. They can experience sensory input in the extreme (hypersensitive) or barely experience the sensory input at all (hyposensitive). If they are hypersensitive to some particular input from their environment, then they will try to avoid it. If they are hyposensitive, they will seek out that sensory stimulation. At times they can be hypersensitive to a certain sense – sound, for example – while being hyposensitive at the same time. So, the hum of the computer may drive them to distraction one day, while the scraping of chalk on the chalk board that sets most peoples' teeth on edge, goes unnoticed. Generally there is consistency in sensory needs, but be aware that they can change from day to day according to mood and other factors.

We have seven senses: vestibular (balance), proprioceptive (body awareness), tactile (touch), visual (sight), auditory (hearing), olfactory (smell) and gustatory (taste).

The vestibular sense (balance)

This is the sense that helps our balance and our spatial awareness. It is important for movement, balance and co-ordination.

> A child who is **hypersensitive** (over-responsive) may be insecure in all activities involving movement including climbing stairs, playing physical games or activities, swinging, jumping, and balancing.

> A child who is **hyposensitive** (under-responsive) may be constantly moving, spinning, jumping, rocking, climbing.

Example of how hypersensitive balance can cause misunderstanding
A young boy walking up the stairs with his class suddenly turned around and grabbed the breasts of a teacher who was coming up close behind him. She was new at the school, didn't know the boy and was outraged. He thought he was about to fall down the stairs and grabbed the first thing that came to hand. The teacher was offended but his experience felt terrifying.

The proprioceptive sense (body awareness)

This is the sense that helps our brain send messages to our body so they know what to do when we want to wriggle our toes or bend our fingers or shake our head without watching what we are doing. It is the sense that helps us know how hard to press with a pencil, or push on a peddle to make it turn, or how to throw a ball.

> A child who is **hypersensitive** will tend to use too much force when using objects which results in paper being torn, objects dropped and broken, writing being too light (so it cannot be seen) or too heavy, tearing clothes when dressing and general clumsiness.

> A child who is **hyposensitive** will seek out the sensation of where their body is in space by banging feet on chairs, toe walking, seeking deep pressure by squeezing into tight spaces, wanting big hugs, jumping on a trampoline, hitting or punching a cushion or person. Deep pressure, carrying heavy weights and pushing and lifting can give some respite.

The tactile sense (touch)

> A child who is **hypersensitive** will react to some sensations as though they are painful. He may dislike being touched anywhere on his body, or will recoil from certain materials like paint or playdough. Some gentle introduction, perhaps with plastic gloves may help overcome tactile defensiveness over time, but never force a child to touch or taste something when he doesn't want to. Offer a variety of tactile experiences and wait and see what happens.

> A child who is **hyposensitive** will seek out certain tactile experiences, sometimes in unlikely places. He may put all kinds of things in his mouth and chew them, or touch certain textures.

Example of how hyposensitive touch can cause misunderstanding
One child on a tube train was fascinated by the black fishnet stockings of the woman sitting opposite. He could not take his eyes off them. Eventually, it became too much to resist and he reached out suddenly and ran his hand up her leg. Luckily, he was young enough not to cause offence on this occasion.

The visual sense (sight)

> A child who is **hypersensitive** may have difficulty coping in areas that have bright colours, fluorescent lights or too many patterns. Of course that will describe many early years centres! Make sure that a child who is disturbed by light or colour has a workstation that has clean, uncluttered neutral walls and work surfaces.

> Children who are **hyposensitive** to light may seek out bright lights and colours and are most motivated by sensory toys that light up, change colour or shimmer.

The auditory sense (hearing)

> A child who is **hypersensitive** will sometimes cover his ears to block out sound because it is so painful. He will be distracted by the hum of a computer, scraping chairs on the floor above, or road works outside.

> A child who is **hyposensitive** often won't respond to sounds or verbal instructions. Sometimes he might make very loud noises because he doesn't realise they are loud. Recognising sound volume can be taught to some extent using visuals.

To help children with auditory sensitivities, use a quiet voice when speaking and recognise that they will need a quiet place to go sometimes. Headphones (if they tolerate them) can help when working at the computer. Ear muffs can sometimes help a little. Being in a noisy environment can create stress that can lead to meltdowns. Always have a safe, soft, quiet corner where children can go to relax.

The olfactory sense (smell)

> A child who is **hypersensitive** may react badly to a certain person because of the perfume she is wearing. He may feel nauseous at the smell of certain food and general smells in the environment including artificial smells in toilets and soap in bathrooms. If you have a child with this problem, don't wear perfume and be aware of what may be causing smells in the toilets at school. He may refuse to use the toilet and sit in discomfort all day, so be aware of this.

> A child who is **hyposensitive** to smell will often seek out smells, sometimes inappropriately, for example wanting to smell a person's skin or hair, or smelling items before using them.

Occupational therapists should assess children with autism and if they have sensory perception issues, a 'sensory diet' will be set up that provides the child with the sensory input that best suits his needs. It is important that the suggestions are followed, even when it takes time away from class work, as the exercises and activities will help the child get through the day much more easily.

The gustatory sense (taste)

> A child who is **hypersensitive** may refuse foods of certain tastes and follow a limited diet consisting of only sweet or bland food, or only certain food prepared the same way each time. It can be very difficult to introduce new foods into his diet and this should be done very gradually, without fuss, following a step-by-step programme. Texture is also an issue that may create eating difficulties and the two are often linked.

> Some children who are **hyposensitive** will sometimes eat all sorts of things including inappropriate substances, food items from the rubbish, or raw food that should be cooked. Again, they may also be seeking the texture of the food as well as the taste.

9. Behaviour support strategies

When working with or caring for children with autism spectrum disorders, it is important to remember that the behaviour you find most difficult to manage is a reflection of difficulties they are experiencing because they have autism.

The most important first step when looking for strategies is to consider the reasons behind the behaviour and to try to understand it from the child's point of view. One of the most obvious reasons for difficult behaviour in children with autism is lack of communication skills. They may not be able to make their needs known, or understand what is expected. This would be very confusing and upsetting for anyone, but especially for a young child.

One of the positive effects of using picture cards, choice boards or PECS (see page 48) to develop communication skills is that it reduces frustration and gives children some control over their environment. However, even children with good verbal skills can have difficulty expressing their needs, feelings and frustrations to another person. Like many of us, when they are very upset, words fail them.

The most important things for you to ask yourself when faced with a situation of anger or unsocial behaviour are:

> 'what is driving this behaviour?'
> 'what is this child trying to tell me?'

Causes of behaviour

There are many reasons for children with autism doing and saying things that we find challenging, unsociable or naughty. Think about the following issues.

Communication difficulties

Does your child want something to stop, or does he want something and is unable to say what it is? Does he understand what you have just said, or what your expectations are? Remember, children with autism may understand your request on a good day, but another day they may be feeling anxious, there is a background computer hum, or they might simply miss the point of what has been said.

Sensory difficulties

Ask yourself: is the situation too loud, too busy, too hot, too cold, too bright, too smelly, too crowded, too uncomfortable or too hard to understand? Is it too much for this child to cope with? What can you do about it?

Lack of social awareness

Are you expecting your child to understand social situations with rules he has not been taught? Does he have the prerequisite skills to behave in the way you expect? Remember that social understanding does not develop naturally for children on the autism spectrum, and they could be very confused by others' behaviour and unaware that their behaviour is inappropriate. Teaching social understanding and good social skills should always be an area that is targeted in any individual education plan.

Rigidity and resistance to change

Has something changed that your child has not been prepared for? For example, roadworks and detours on the way to school, specific food items being unavailable, changes to schedule and people in the classroom, different clothes, new wall displays, unexpected weather conditions or unfamiliar demands. Very small, subtle changes can feel like the end of the world and lead to meltdowns that are unexpected and hard to avoid. Sometimes these things have no answer except understanding and calm in the face of extreme distress. But whenever possible, try to limit change and prepare for known changes in advance.

General upsets

A child may be feeling unwell, lacking sleep, there may be stress at home, he may be hungry or thirsty, or simply having a bad day. If he is unusually upset or angry, check that he does not have a temperature or that he is not rubbing an ear or his tummy. Always have a home and school book and encourage parents to write in it if he has a sleepless night, or if something changes at home. Maybe Grandma has gone on holiday, or the sitting room has been redecorated or the furniture has been moved. Some children won't react at all to these events, others will become so anxious it affects all their behaviour.

If it is not clear what the cause is, it can be helpful to record the following information on a STAR chart:

> **S**etting: when the behaviour occurs and who is present at the time
> **T**rigger: what happened immediately before the incident
> **A**ction: description of the incident
> **R**esponse: what happened next?

A pattern may emerge that should give some idea of what is causing the behaviour and then strategies can be put in place to try and put it right. Sometimes, there are several reasons and these can be difficult to disentangle but look for one or two main reasons that become obvious as a result of analysis and can provide a starting point to make a plan.

In the example below, it does not take much to work out what is happening.

Finn is six years old and was moved to a resourced school from a mainstream school. His diagnosis of autism is recent. He is verbal and can make his needs known but a lot of his language is delayed echolalia. He was very anxious however, and often sat crying at carpet time when he came in from lunch. He is very sensitive to change and reacts badly to noise and bustle.

His response to being in the playground for too long was to take off his shoes and throw them where they could not be retrieved in a hurry, as the premises officer was on his break. He realised if he did this, he would be taken inside to the quiet. The solution? He was taken indoors every day at 12.30 for quiet indoor play with a small group of peers. That was the short-term strategy. The longer-term strategy was to teach him to use a symbol on a keyring to indicate that he needs to go to a quiet place. He had a Social Story™ and the use of the symbol was modelled for him over many days. Gradually, within months, he was able to stay outside for longer periods playing with his peers.

STAR Chart for Finn

Setting	Trigger	Action	Response
10/05 12.40 KS1 Playground boat area with LA Amy.	Playing on boat.	Threw trainers on roof.	Told off, taken inside with no shoes, time out.
12/05 12.30 KS1 Playground with LA Amy.	Standing with a group of boys.	Pulled off trainers and threw over wall.	Told off, told his parents will be cross. Sent to time out, no more play.
16/05 12.39 KS1 Playground with Julia.	Playing in sand with two other boys (Jamie, Luke).	Threw hat and sand bucket showering sand everywhere.	Told off, taken to Deputy to sit in her office. Note to parents.
24/05 12.20 KS1 Playground with Julia.	Sitting in noisy boat area looking at books.	Threw one trainer over the wall.	Taken to apologise to premises officer who has to fetch his shoe during lunch break. Stays indoors.
26/05 12.35 KS1 Playground boat area with LA Julia.	Noisy play around him.	Threw trainers on shed roof.	Told off, taken into class and given work to do. Email parents.

There are several other important points to keep in mind when you want to change a child's behaviour.

> **Be positive.** Use rewards for acceptable behaviour rather than sanctions for unacceptable behaviour.

> **Be patient.** Whatever strategy you decide to follow will not work immediately. Wait at least four weeks, particularly with a very young child, before deciding to try something else. Some strategies, such as developing a method of communication, are very long term and need to be broken into small steps, especially for children who have additional learning needs.

> **Be consistent.** Make sure that everybody who spends time with the child knows how to respond to the target behaviour and sticks to the strategy.

> **Be calm!** An angry or loud response might help you feel better, but it is unlikely to help a child who may be confused and/ or sensitive to loud noises.

> **Be creative.** Do not be afraid to try new ideas if you think they might work.

Behaviour that hurts other children – biting or pushing for example – can rightly upset parents. All you can do is explain what you have decided to do about it and hope that parents will understand in the long run. Many young children can suddenly bite or push another if they feel sufficiently upset, but persistent biting and pushing where safety is an issue can be harder to deal with. Look for alternative spaces in school. Consider whether the child in question is ready for constant exposure to groups and all the sensory, social and communication skills that involves. Look for alternatives, find quiet corners, develop rituals and routines, stay very calm, ride the storm and it will pass.

Some strategies are difficult to put into practice in mainstream schools. These include finding motivating rewards, acquiring a quiet spot in a crowded playground, ignoring screaming or other noises, providing a quiet, calm environment, having enough staff to set up alternative arrangements for a child who is struggling. Flexibility, training for all staff, co-operative work with parents and other professionals and a willingness to make inclusion work are all important factors in helping a child with an autism spectrum disorder succeed in school. It may also be necessary to provide circle time sessions with classes to help all young children understand that we are different, and that some of their peers may need a little extra understanding.

Behaviour support strategies: some examples

Example 1
Tolu has been in nursery for six weeks and has no additional adult support.

He has limited vocabulary and does not interact with the other children. If they come near him or try to join in with what he is doing, he pushes them hard out of his way.

Possible reasons for Tolu's behaviour are that:

> other children are unpredictable and he finds them frightening
> the environment is too stimulating (too loud or too busy)
> he likes hearing his peers cry
> he likes the attention he gets when he hurts someone
> he does not know how to play or interact with his peers
> he does not understand that when he gives another child a turn, he will have a turn himself later.

Short-term strategies to try are:

> if Tolu hurts another child, saying calmly, 'No pushing. Be gentle' and showing him what 'gentle' means by stroking his hand lightly
> taking him to a quiet area for some 'down' time with music or sensory toys
> trying to get extra support for Tolu so that he can be taught to play with his peers
> for big things, such as taking turns on the trike, using a timer so that Tolu can see when it is time to change.

Long-term strategies:

> teaching Tolu to take turns with an adult (see Chapter 1, page 29)
> teaching Tolu to wait using a wait card (see Chapter 2, page 57)
> trying the strategies regularly – it will take time for Tolu to change his behaviour.

Example 2
Amber is three and has been at playgroup for six weeks. She has severe communication difficulties but, given extra adult support, has begun to use a variety of materials and equipment.

However, Amber likes to throw toys in the air. This is dangerous and the toys often hit other children or knock things over.

Possible reasons for Amber's behaviour are that:

> she does not understand that she may hurt someone or what that means for the other children
> she has no sense of safety, for herself or for others
> she does not know how to play, interact or communicate with others
> she may find the noise and activity around her makes her feel uncomfortable and throwing a toy calms her
> she has a sensory need (proprioceptive) to throw something heavy in the air.

Short-term strategies to try are:

> when Amber is throwing toys, picking them up and showing her how to play with them
> if it is a doll, for example, saying 'No throwing, cuddle dolly' and model the positive behaviour
> teaching Amber to throw a small beanbag or soft ball to an adult as a turn-taking game, or into a bucket or net
> if Amber keeps throwing toys, taking them away and taking her to sit in a quiet area for a few minutes, then distracting her with another activity
> trying to provide some structure to Amber's time at playgroup by having a structured play session with an adult, outside playtime, relaxation time, story-time, drink and snack time, and introducing a visual timetable using symbols.

Long-term strategies to try are:

> trying to get an occupational therapist to assess Amber's sensory needs, but if this takes too long you could try doing fun exercises with her that provide deep pressure, like rolling her tightly in a blanket, using a weighted blanket or vest, or giving her a weighted backpack to carry on an 'errand' – and doing these activities once or twice a day
> teaching Amber play skills by having an adult modelling and prompting play routines, then inviting another child to join in.

Example 3
Suzie has moved up to reception from nursery.

She has settled in well but will not use the toilet, even when it is clear that she wants to go. The toilets are used by several classes and are bigger and busier than the little toilets in the nursery.

Suzie will use the nursery toilet but, when she is taken back to the nursery, she wants to stay there and becomes so distressed it is hard to move her on to anything else.

Possible reasons for Suzie's behaviour are that:

> she is upset by the change of class and is unable to use the bigger toilets
> she does not like the smell or sounds in the bigger toilets – for example, there is a hot air dryer that is very noisy
> it is a ploy to go back to the nursery.

Short-term strategies to try are:

> taking Suzie to the staff toilet at a quiet time and seeing if she will go there; it is common for children with autism spectrum disorders to find the sound of hot air dryers and flushing toilets very frightening
> taking Suzie to visit the girls' toilets twice a day when it is quiet, but not asking her to use the toilet, only to look at what is there or wash her hands if she will allow this
> gradually building up the time spent there, and, when she seems confident, encouraging her to use the toilet
> building a time to go to the toilet into her timetable
> setting a time for Suzie to visit the nursery and putting it on her timetable so that she knows she can still visit and when she can do so
> rewarding Suzie when she uses the toilet.

Long-term strategy

Develop a programme that will accustom Suzie to sudden loud noises in small steps, so that she no longer fears the hand dryer or toilet flush.

Example 4

Geetha is in the reception class. She has limited vocabulary and has a helper all the time. When she goes to PE, she runs very fast around the hall and does not follow instructions.

Possible reasons for Geetha's behaviour are that:

> the hall is large and echoes and she has difficulty understanding and following instructions
> the hall has no structure and no boundaries, so she does not know how to structure her time when she is in it
> she loves to run around
> she does not understand the games and activities the class are asked to do in PE.

Short-term strategies to try are:

> having a mat that is Geetha's place and taking her there when the children are told to find a space
> using gestures to help Geetha understand what she has to do
> getting her to practise sitting in the hall – tell her to 'Sit first, then run'
> giving her a lot of praise for good responses
> holding her gently from behind to give her a physical boundary when the children are sitting on the floor
> modelling for her what she should do and using physical and verbal prompts to help her.

Long-term strategies to try are:

> using large symbols for 'walk', 'run', 'stop', 'sit' and teaching Geetha what they mean
> increasing expectations one step at a time.

Example 5

Joe is in the reception class. He has a helper from 9.30am until 2.30pm and works well with her in the morning.

In the afternoon, though, he does not co-operate and frequently loses his temper, hitting anybody who comes near. His behaviour is unpredictable and there is a real concern that somebody will be badly hurt, so he is frequently sent home at 2.30pm when his helper goes.

Possible reasons for Joe's behaviour are that:

> he does not like the school dinners – the school is trying to encourage healthy eating and does not allow children to bring a packed lunch, and consequently, Joe does not eat lunch
> the afternoon is less structured and noisier than the morning and children do more play-based activities, such as construction, sand and water play – Joe may be sensitive to the sound and movement or confused by the lack of structure in the classroom
> he is very active and may be feeling tired by the afternoon.

Short-term strategies to try are:

> making sure that Joe has something he likes at lunchtime, even if it is brought from home – children with autism do not like change and are also sensitive to some smells and textures of food, but can be gradually encouraged to eat a wider diet after settling down at school
> when the children are doing less structured activities early in the afternoon, taking Joe out or to a quiet corner of the classroom to do a structured TEACCH session where he could practise skills and games he knows well with adult support
> finding a relaxing activity for Joe to do at the end of the day when his helper has gone, for example, listening to music, computer activities, or playing with sensory toys
> re-arranging the helper's hours so that he has less time when he is unsupported at the end of the day.

Long-term strategies to try are:

> addressing Joe's difficulty with developing play ideas and playing with others by getting him to practise these skills, first with an adult modelling, and then with one or two other children
> gradually and gently encouraging Joe to try new food items – try simple cooking sessions or games for feeding dolly – then trying it himself and never force him to taste something against his will.

Example 6
Lily is a preverbal child in the reception class. She likes playing in the sand but she always throws it up so that it blows in children's eyes and hair. Usually she is told off when this happens and is taken away from the sand.

Possible reasons for Lily's behaviour are that:

> she likes to watch the sand as it falls down in a fine shower
> she enjoys the fuss she creates when the sand goes in children's eyes
> throwing the sand is relaxing to Lily and it distracts her from the noisy play environment
> having limited play skills, she is pleased she has found something she enjoys.

Short-term strategies to try are:

> writing a Social Story™ and reading it to Lily before play
> using a very motivating reward when Lily does not throw sand
> saying 'No throwing' and show a symbol, then taking her away from the sand without giving any attention
> using a schedule to show Lily when she can play in the sand – make this a time when her peers are elsewhere, so you can be very clear when she throws it saying 'No sand, sand finished!', take her away and show her that it is over by adjusting her schedule.

Long-term strategy

Spend time teaching Lily how to play with other equipment and toys in the playground.

Example 7

Shenelle is in the reception class. She has good language skills and, when the children are on the carpet, she always calls out the answer without raising her hand. She also makes comments in a loud voice that are not relevant to the lesson.

Possible reasons for Shenelle's behaviour are that:

> she does not remember that she always has to raise her hand and wait to be asked the answer – it confuses her when she is not always chosen every time she raises her hand
> she does not understand the social context of having a conversation, so she will say what she wants when it comes into her head.

Short-term strategies to try are:

> writing a Social Story™ for Shenelle about what happens when the children are sitting on the carpet and what she should do
> having a reward system for Shenelle so that she can earn a reward when she has managed not to call out on the carpet – the reward could be something she enjoys, such as using the computer for ten minutes
> having a visual notice using drawings on the wall near the teacher to remind children to raise their hands and wait their turn to be chosen – if Shenelle speaks out, pointing to the notice and saying, 'Raise your hand and wait to be chosen'.

Long-term strategies to try are:

> teaching Shenelle to wait using a 'wait' card (Chapter 2, page 57)
> teaching Shenelle turn-taking and waiting games.

Example 8

Adam is in Year one. He is obsessed with flags and can name and draw the flags of most countries in the world. However, he will not talk about anything else and will often talk about flags when he is supposed to be working.

Possible reasons for Adam's behaviour are that:

> talking about flags makes him feel calm
> he does not understand that flags are not interesting to others
> he does not have social conversation skills and cannot join in the chat that happens between his peers.

Short-term strategies to try are:

> giving Adam a written schedule for the day including the times that he is allowed to talk about flags, and using it as a reward for finishing his work
> writing a Social Story™ explaining when Adam can talk about flags
> using a timer so that Adam knows how long he has to talk about flags
> being firm with Adam and reminding him when it is the wrong time to talk about flags – 'Work first, then flags'
> using flags to teach Adam things he may find difficult, such as maths, or to teach him other things about the countries they are from.

Long-term strategy

Play games with Adam that will encourage him to listen to others. For example, try a conversation game where each child is given the first line and they have to take turns to keep the conversation going. Alternatively, use circle time to check that the children are listening to each other by choosing a child and asking what was just said.

Example 9

Jamie is in Year one. He is coping well academically but hates getting wet. If he gets wet when he is washing his hands or splashing in a puddle he will pull all his clothes off wherever he is and run about with no clothes on. This behaviour also happens at home. He is very sensitive to certain textures and refuses to wear waterproof aprons or overalls.

Possible reasons for Jamie's behaviour are that:

> he does not understand that it is not acceptable to run about naked
> he is hypersensitive to the touch of wet clothing and cannot stand it near his skin
> he does not know what to do when he gets wet.

Short-term strategies to try are:

> talking to Jamie's peers about what they can do to help him, such as fetching an adult, taking him in to the toilets and so on
> writing a Social Story™ for Jamie, telling him what to do if he gets wet
> teaching Jamie how to change his wet clothes using the TEACCH method (see Chapter 3, page 71): keep a basket of clothes for Jamie in the toilets or some other suitable place where he can reach them and teach him what to do step by step by wetting his clothes and showing him how to change them
> having buddies for Jamie who know what to do and can support him if it happens.

Long-term strategy

Build up Jamie's resistance to coping with wet clothing by dampening his clothes a little bit and have him wait before being able to change them. Try distraction, very motivating rewards, lots of praise, using a wait card and so on. Do this regularly and build up the time that he has to wait.

> **Example 10**
> Belle is in Year two. She has recently been diagnosed with Asperger syndrome. She is very tactless and upsets other children so they do not want to play with her. She takes what she wants without asking, so, for example, if she wants a pencil, she will snatch it from another child's hand. Recently she was found crying in the playground because she had no friends to play with.

Possible reasons for Belle's behaviour are that:

> she lacks social understanding and social interaction skills – she cannot imagine how other children feel when she upsets them
> she may not know what to do in the playground and may feel lost and confused in an unstructured setting.

Short-term strategies to try are:

> writing a Social Story™ about how to act in certain situations including what Belle should do when she is in a group – sharing a pot of pencils would be one example
> setting up a lunchtime club and teaching playground games, board games, sharing games and so on
> setting up a circle of friends for Belle (see Chapter 6, page 110).

Long-term strategy

Do some work with Belle on understanding emotions using picture cards, photographs and real situations. Use 'Why? Because' cards (see Useful resources, page 152) to help Belle understand some social situations. For example, talk about what is happening in a picture and try to think what might have happened before and why, then what will happen after and why. Use art, drama and role play to explore feelings and how to behave in social situations.

Example 11

Harry is in Year two. He has attention deficit hyperactivity disorder (ADHD) and autism. He has previously gone home at lunchtime because he has difficulty coping in the unstructured, noisy playground. Now he is in Year two, he is going to have lunch at school with adult support. The school has set up a lunchtime club for Harry with a small group of other children who have difficulties with social interaction, and Harry has had this explained to him. However, whenever Harry is taken into the dining room, he lashes out at nearby children and throws his food on the floor. He refuses to eat and his peers are afraid of him.

Possible reasons for Harry's behaviour are that:

> he finds the dining room too bright and noisy and there is too much activity, he feels afraid and panics
> he does not understand why he has to stay at school for lunchtime and is confused
> he doesn't like the look and smell of the food
> he is having difficulty accepting the change to his routine.

Strategies to try are:

> writing a Social Story™ about what happens in the dining room at lunchtime and reading it to Harry before lunch, using photos if possible showing positive role models
> showing Harry his timetable and reminding him during the morning that he is having lunch at school
> if possible taking Harry to the dining hall a little before his peers so that he can settle while it is still quiet
> discussing Harry's likes and dislikes with his parents and asking them to look at the menu, so that you know in advance what Harry would prefer to eat
> looking into an exception being made for Harry to allow him to have a packed lunch from home and access to school meals if he wants them
> asking Harry to choose what he wants from the menu before going to the dining hall
> working out whether Harry might cope better having his lunch at a table in a quiet area outside the dining area – when he can manage this calmly, gradually move the table nearer to the dining room; when he can manage sitting inside the door of the dining room, ask him to choose a friend to sit beside him, then join his table together with another table (this process may take several weeks and should be worked through at a pace that suits him)
> in the longer term, encouraging Harry to taste unfamiliar food by giving cooking or sensory lessons involving food.

Example 12

Amy is in Year two. She has full-time support and her timetable is differentiated to meet her needs.

She has limited communication skills and sometimes screams or cries and refuses to work. This disrupts the class and disturbs the teacher. She has to be taken out of the class when this happens, but there is nowhere to go except the playground or passageway.

Possible reasons for Amy's behaviour are that:

> she uses screaming to avoid working
> she is confused about what she has to do, or her work is too hard
> she does not know how to ask for help
> she has 'sensory overload' because there is too much sensory input for her to cope with, so she becomes distraught and needs to leave the room
> she enjoys the attention she gets by screaming.

Short-term strategies to try are:

> using a visual timetable and structuring Amy's work, showing her that when she has finished she can go outside to run around
> using a visual 'quiet' symbol to remind her not to make a noise
> being sensitive to her moods – if she is becoming agitated, try taking her to wash her hands or walk to the office then back to the classroom to do some more work (giving a work break)
> presenting the tasks she has to do in a clear, visual way so that she is not confused by too much information (see Chapter 3: structured teaching, page 71)
> alternating fun activities with more difficult ones
> offering more choices during work time, for example choosing from two worksheets or activities or choosing reading books

Quiet

> offering frequent, positive and motivating rewards for finishing work
> when she is taken out of class, always bringing her back to the unfinished work
  (or taking it with you) even if you have to finish it more quickly
> not giving attention to the screaming – don't talk to her or make a fuss about it.

Long-term strategies to try are:

> teaching Amy relaxation using modelling and a visual Social Story™
> teaching Amy to say when she is feeling overwhelmed by using an 'I need a break'
  card – but restricting the number of break cards that are available.

Although behaviour support strategies may take days or weeks to succeed, it is important to be consistent as much as possible and ensure that everyone working with or caring for the child knows what the agreed response to certain behaviour should be. Parents, carers and school staff have to work together or the child will become confused and the behaviour you are trying to change could get worse. It is also worth remembering that if a child is used to getting attention by screaming, for example, and you withdraw that attention, the immediate response from the child will be to scream more loudly!

When you are planning your strategies you should remember that for a day or two at least, things could get worse. However, it can be most rewarding when a short time later, things start to get better and within six weeks you may well have forgotten there was a problem.

Some final thoughts

This book of ideas and suggestions is by no means complete. The aim has been to write a book long enough to be useful but not so long that you lose interest! A good book cannot replace good training and experience but it can be a useful prop and point of reference when difficulties arise.

The importance of 'joined-up working' (all professionals, parents and carers working together and keeping each other informed) cannot be stressed enough. Make sure information about what has happened in school and what is happening at home goes back and forth on a regular basis. This makes such a difference to the level of progress that is possible and can mean all kinds of damaging mistakes can be avoided.

Teachers, nursery officers and play leaders must work hard to get to know the children with autism spectrum disorders as well as they know the other children in their class or nursery. Support workers are often on the front line, working closely with the children every day, but they should be supported by teachers and other colleagues, not left feeling isolated.

Special educational needs co-ordinators (SENCOs) also play an important role in ensuring that targets are set, reviews are carried out on time, training is organised and awareness is raised generally throughout the school.

Other professionals – who may include clinical and educational psychologists, speech and language therapists, specialist teachers and occupational therapists – should ensure that they know who is involved with the child and what advice is being given by different people. All reports about individual children should be discussed with parents, including behaviour plans, individual education plans, speech and language and occupational therapy programmes, and information about learning goals.

Working with children with autism is very rewarding. Keep at it!

References

Baron-Cohen, S. (1995). *Mindblindness*. Cambridge, Massachusetts: MIT Press

Baron-Cohen, S., and Bolton, P. (1993). *Autism: The Facts*. Oxford: Oxford University Press*

Beyer, J., and Gammeltoft, L. (2000). *Autism and Play*. London: Jessica Kingsley*

Cauldwell, P. and Horwood, J. (2008). *Using Intensive Interaction and Sensory Integration*. London: Jessica Kingsley

Goldbart, J. (1988). Re-examining the Development of Early Communication. in Coupe, J. and Goldbart, J. ed. (1988). *Communication Before Speech: Normal development and impaired communication*. Beckenham, Kent: Croom Helm

Gray, C. (1997). *Social Stories and Comic Strip Conversations*. Arlington, Texas: Future Horizons (available in the UK from Winslow)

Grandin, T. (1995). *Thinking in Pictures and other Reports from my Life with Autism*. New York: Vintage Books*

Jordan, R. and Jones, G. (1999). *Meeting the Needs of Children with Autistic Spectrum Disorders. London*: David Fulton*

Newman, S. (1999). *Small Steps Forward*. London: Jessica Kingsley*

Newton, C. and Wilson, D. (1999). *Circles of Friends*. Dunstable: Folens Ltd

Sussman, F. (1999). *More than Words*. Ontario: The Hanen Centre

*Available from NAS Publications. For more information email **publications@nas.org.uk**.

The National Autistic Society EarlyBird Programme
EarlyBird Centre, Barnsley Road, Dodworth, South Yorkshire S75 3JT

Phone: **01226 779218**
Email: **earlybird@nas.org.uk**
Website: **www.autism.org.uk/earlybird**

Division TEACCH (Treatment and Education of Autistic and related Communication handicapped Children), Administration and Research
CB 7180, 310 Medical School Wing E, University of North Carolina at Chapel Hill, Chapel Hill, North Carolina, 27599-7180 USA

Phone: **+001 (919) 966 2174**
Email: **TEACCH@unc.edu**
Website: **teacch.com**

For more information about TEACCH, visit
www.autism.org.uk/living-with-autism/strategies-and-approaches/teacch.

Further reading

Attwood, T. (1997). *Asperger Syndrome: A guide for parents and professionals*. London: Jessica Kingsley

Berger, A. and Gross, J. (1999). *Teaching the Literacy Hour in an Inclusive Classroom*. London: David Fulton

Berger, A., Henderson, J., and Morris, D. (1999). *Implementing the Literacy Hour for Pupils with Learning Difficulties*. London: David Fulton

Cumine, V., Leach, J., and Stevenson, G. (1997). *Asperger Syndrome: A practical guide for teachers. London*: David Fulton

Detheridge, T. and Detheridge, M. (1997). *Literacy Through Symbols: Improving access for children and adults*. London: David Fulton

Gillingham, G. (1995). *Autism, Handle with Care*. Arlington, Texas: Future Horizons

Gray, C. (1993). *The Original Social Story Book*. Arlington, Texas: Future Horizons (available in the UK from Winslow, Chesterfield, Derbyshire)

Wall, K. (2009). *Autism and Early Years Practice*. London: Sage Publications

Lear, R. (1996). *Play Helps*. Oxford: Butterworth Heinemann

Leicester City Council and Leicestershire County Council (1998). *Asperger Syndrome – Practical Strategies for the Classroom: A teacher's guide*. London: The National Autistic Society

Leicestershire County Council and Fosse Health Trust (1998). *Autism: How to help your young child*. London: The National Autistic Society

Lynch, C. and Cooper, J. (1991). *Early Communication Skills*. Bicester, Oxfordshire: Winslow Press (new edition available from Winslow)

Powell, S. and Jordan, R. (1997). *Autism and Learning: A guide to good practice*. London: David Fulton

Williams, D. (1996). *Autism: An inside-out approach*. London: Jessica Kingsley

Useful resources

Websites

Autism Sparks: www.autismsparks.com
This website contains hints, information and ideas for parents and teachers. It is run by a teacher of children with autism and has many useful tips in addition to a section about autism.

TES Resources: www.tes.co.uk/teaching-resources
This is a wonderful site containing a huge number of free resources that have been posted by teachers and others working in education. There is a section just for special needs, but the early years' section is also full of useful visual resources.

Twinkl: www.twinkl.co.uk
This contains some excellent free and inexpensive visual resources for use in the classroom or at home, with a section specifically for children with autism. The site also has a vast range of visual teaching resources on curriculum topics.

SEN Teacher: www.senteacher.org/print/aac/
This site is the best place to go for free symbols and photographs. You can print them in colour in three different sizes and they are great for images showing different cultures and different celebrations. They also have fans you can print showing emotions, and quick to use visual aids, including 'yes', 'no', 'I need a break', traffic lights, numeracy concepts and many more.

Communication 4 All: www.communication4all.co.uk
Colourful resources to support inclusion, including free music videos, story packs, literacy and numeracy resources supported by symbols, and simple games that can be printed and laminated. Some of the resources cost a small amount but many are free.

Makaton: www.makaton.org
A system of signs and symbols. Particularly good for singing and simple story telling, the site has many free resources, information about training courses in Makaton, and simple, inexpensive books that include Makaton signs and symbols along with stories and rhymes. They also sell DVDs based on the Mr Tumble BBC series *Something Special* using signs and symbols to support fun songs and stories.

Sensory Direct: www.sensorydirect.com
This is a good place to go if you need weighted wrist bands, chew toys for children who seek chewing stimulation, weighted blankets and vests for those needing proprioceptive input.

PECS (Picture Exchange Communication System): www.pecs-unitedkingdom.com
Very useful for information about courses or to buy visual resources, motivating toys, PECS books and other information relating to PECS.

Autism Apps: www.touchautism.com/app/autism-apps
This is a list of apps that are being used with people diagnosed with autism and other special needs. It includes links to any available information that can be found for each app. The apps are separated into categories, and the descriptions are all searchable, so any type of app is easy to find and download.

Software

Communicate in Print 2: www.widgit.com
Developing communication, language and literacy with pictures, symbols and words. This easy to use software includes symbols from the Rebus symbols collection and the Picture Communication Symbols.

Proloquo2Go by AssistiveWare: www.assistiveware.com/product/proloquo2go
This software for iPad and iPhone is a comprehensive communication aid for a child with autism and many schools are using it. However, as it is expensive, best to discuss it with your speech and language therapist before purchase. It is available to purchase on iTunes.

Other resources

Pocket ColorCards: Available from www.speechmark.net
Pocket-sized sets of language flashcards, including early objects, actions, sequences and opposites. An excellent resource for developing language skills.

ColorCards: Basic Sequences/Simple Sequences: Available from
www.speechmark.net
These photo cards show simple, three-step sequences of routine events to help develop language and sequencing skills.

Emotions Photocards: Available from www.taskmasteronline.co.uk
51 pairs of photocards showing emotions, 15 pairs of black and white cards and four mirrors. A great resource to help with talking about and recognising feelings.

Tell About It: Available from www.ldalearning.com
A set of 26 picture stories designed to encourage children to sequence, predict and tell a story. Each sequence has four, five, six or seven cards.

Why? Because cards: Available from www.ldalearning.com
Each pair of picture cards depicts a situation that can be used to sequence, to predict what happens next or what happened before and as the starting point to develop a simple story. They provide good practice for answering questions and making inferences.

My friend Sam: a story about introducing a child with autism to nursery school
Available from www.autism.org.uk/shop.
An accessible picture book uses simple wording and colour pictures to describe some of the difficulties that young children with autism may have, and also some of the things they are very good at.

Index

A

adding, teaching of   104-5
activity books, for numeracy   103
aggression *see* pushing; throwing things
arithmetic *see* numeracy
asking for things   39-41
    encouraging   41-44
    see also choices
assemblies   55-56
attention, developing   60-62
autistic children
    areas of difficulty   9-12
    educational provision   7
awareness, of other children   82-85, 108, 133

B

backward chaining   67-68
behaviour support   130
    examples   132-145
behaviours
    recording   131-32
    see also social behaviour
books
    developing interest in   89-91
    for language development   46
    see also interactive books;
    reading; stories
breath control, development of   33
buddy systems   108-9
    see also circle of friends
bullying, prevention of   108-9

Index

C

capital letters, in handwriting   97
chaining   67-68
change, resistance to *see* flexible thinking
choices
    offering   37-39
    see also asking for things
circle of friends   110-112
circle time   109
classroom disruption *see* disruption
classroom skills, developing   61-62, 144-45
communication
    problems   9-10, 139-140
    see also home-school communication;
    Picture Exchange Communication System
communication skills
    in play   14-20
    songs for   16, 21-22, 29, 32-33, 35-37
    through environmental adaptation   39-40
    see also choices; eye contact; feelings;
    language development; signs; symbols;
    turn-taking
computer skills   99
concentration, developing   60-62
conversations, development of   43-45, 140-41
copying *see* imitation
counting activities   100-1
creativity, developing   120
cursive writing, teaching   97

D

dice, for numeracy   104-5
disruption, avoiding   62, 119-20, 144-45

E

early intervention, value   7
EarlyBird programme   147
eating problems   143

educational provision, for autistic children	7
emotions, understanding	112-114
environmental adaptation, for communication skills	39-41
eye contact, development of	27-29

F

failure, fear of	98, 116
feelings, understanding	112-114
flexible thinking	
development of	117-24
problems with	9-12, 68
food rewards	52-53
forward chaining	67
friends *see* interactive play; peer support;	
playmates; relationships	

G

games *see* PE; play	
generalising skills	68-70, 76-78
groups	
sitting in	55-56
stories in	90-91
working in	78-79, 109, 139

H

handwriting, development of	95-98
home-school communication	70
hyperlexia	91

I

imagination *see* flexible thinking; pretend play	
imitation skills, development of	36, 63-66
independent work, developing	78-79, 116
instructions, techniques for	61-62, 137
interactive play	18-20, 27, 85, 118
see also turn-taking	

K

keyboard skills   99
knowledge, generalising   68-69

L

labelling, for literacy   92
language development   41-5, 121
    see also conversations; sound making
literacy *see* books; handwriting; reading; stories
lunchtime clubs   109

M

matching activities   79, 90-91, 92, 100-1
mathematics *see* numeracy
mind, theory of   112
mistakes, fear of   98, 116
modelling   65-66
morning routines, schedules for   79-81
motivation building   58-59
    see also rewards
mouth, awareness of   33
music *see* songs

N

number lines   105
number songs   101-3
numeracy, development of   100-6
nurseries, structured teaching in   82-87

O

obsessions, strategies for   119-20
oral awareness   33
outdoor play   23

P

PE, strategies for 137
peer support 108-12
pencil skills 96-97
personal hygiene, routines 75, 79, 135-37
photographs *see* symbols
physical education *see* PE
physical skills, teaching 65-67
pictorial choice boards 38, 40
Picture Exchange Communication System 48-50
pictures *see* symbols
play
    developing 15-27, 84-85, 117-18, 134-35, 138-39
    making time for 26
    see also obsessions
playground support 108-12
playgroups, structured teaching in 82-87
playmates 26
poetry 91
see also rhymes; songs
praise
    use of 52-53
    see also rewards
pretend play, developing 84-85
prompting 79
puppet play 23
pushing, dealing with 14, 15, 134

Q

questions, techniques for 56

R

reading
    development of 47-48, 91-94
    see also books; stories
relationships, development of 13-26
relaxation tapes 37
requesting *see* asking

resourced schools   7

rewards, use of   52-53, 59, 60, 77, 78-79

rhymes

    for play   21-22

    see also poetry; songs

rigidity of thought *see* flexible thinking

rough and tumble play   18-20

routines

    flexibility in   81,119

    see also schedules

S

sand throwing   138

schedules   59, 72-75, 76-77, 79-81, 83

schools *see* nurseries; resourced schools; specialist units

sequencing skills   94

shaping   66

sharing *see* turn-taking

signs

    use of   46-47

    see also symbols

sitting down, teaching   54-57, 84

skills, generalising   68-70, 77-78

social behaviour, inappropriate   141

social interaction

    development of skills   107-16, 143

    problems with   9-11

    through language   43-45

    see also feelings; interactive play;

    obsessions; turn-taking; waiting

social stories   114-16

songs

    for communication skills   23, 32-37, 39

    for numeracy   101-3

    for play development   16, 21

    for turn-taking   32, 36

    see also poetry; rhymes

sorting activities   86-87

sound making, development of   34

special interests *see* obsessions

specialist units   7

stamping activities, for numeracy   104

stories

      for developing pretend play   118

      writing   120

      see also books; social stories

structured teaching   71

      activities   86-87

      case studies   76-85, 138, 144

      in nurseries   82-87

      see also schedules

swinging rhymes   21

symbols   46-50, 62, 83

      for choices   37-39

      and reading development   92-94

      in schedules   73

      for waiting   58

      see also visual prompts

symbols programs   48, 83

T

talking *see* conversations; language development

target setting   51, 84-85

TEACCH   71, 148

theory of mind   112-13

throwing things   134-35, 138

tickling rhymes   22

timetables *see* schedules

toilet routines   75, 135-36

tongue, awareness of   33

toy throwing   134-35

triad of impairments   9-11

turn-taking, development of   29-33, 36, 45

U

units, in mainstream schools 7

V

visual prompts
    for conversation 44
    see also symbols
vocabulary development 42-43
see also words

W

waiting, teaching 57-58, 139-40
washing *see* personal hygiene
water play 22-23
words
    understanding the meaning of 92-94, 98, 121
    see also vocabulary development
writing *see* handwriting; stories

Notes